FEMINIST APPROACHES TO THE BIBLE

D0074439

ON THE COVER: "Miriam" by Shraga Weil is a detail from the ceiling in the Israel Lounge at the Kennedy Center for the Performing Arts in Washington, D.C. Weil's ceiling is a complex panorama of biblical scenes celebrating musical themes. "Then Miriam the prophet...took timbrel in her hand, and all the women went out after her." *Photo ©Pucker Gallery, Boston.*

FEMINIST APPROACHES TO THE BIBLE

Symposium at the Smithsonian Institution
September 24, 1994

Sponsored by the Resident Associate Program

❦

PHYLLIS TRIBLE

TIKVA FRYMER-KENSKY

PAMELA J. MILNE

JANE SCHABERG

HERSHEL SHANKS, MODERATOR

❦

Biblical Archaeology Society
Washington, DC

Library of Congress Cataloging-in-Publication Data
Feminist approaches to the Bible: symposium at the
Smithsonian Institution, September 24, 1994 /
Phyllis Trible...[et al]; Hershel Shanks, moderator.
p. cm.
Includes bibliographical references.
1. Bible—Feminist criticism—Congresses.
I. Trible, Phyllis. II. Shanks, Hershel. III. Smithsonian Institution.
BS521.4.F44 1995 220.6′082—dc20 95-21064
ISBN 1-880317-41-9

Designed by Auras Design, Washington, DC

©1995 Biblical Archaeology Society
4710 41st Street, NW
Washington, DC 20016

Table of Contents

Participants

Hershel Shanks, moderator, is editor of *Biblical Archaeology Review* and *Bible Review*. He is also the editor and author of many books, including *Understanding the Dead Sea Scrolls* (Random House, 1992) and *Jerusalem: An Archaeological Biography* (Random House, 1995).

Phyllis Trible is Baldwin Professor of Sacred Literature at Union Theological Seminary in New York. She is the author of *God and the Rhetoric of Sexuality* (Fortress Press, 1978), *Texts of Terror: Literary Feminist Readings of Biblical Narratives* (Fortress Press, 1984) and *Rhetorical Criticism: Context, Method, and The Book of Jonah* (Fortress Press, 1994).

Tikva Frymer-Kensky is professor of Hebrew Bible at the Divinity School of the University of Chicago and director of biblical studies at the Reconstructionist Rabbinical College in Philadelphia. Her publications include *In the Wake of the Goddesses* (Free Press, 1992) and *The Judicial Ordeal in the Ancient Near East* (Styx, 1995).

Pamela J. Milne is associate professor of Hebrew Bible at the University of Windsor, Ontario, and the author of an introduction and annotation for the Book of Daniel in *The NRSV: Harper's Study Edition* (HarperCollins, 1993) and "The Patriarchal Stamp of Scripture" (*Journal of Feminist Studies in Religion*, 1989).

Jane Schaberg is professor of religious studies at the University of Detroit–Mercy, where she has taught since 1977. A specialist in the New Testament, Schaberg is the author of *The Illegitimacy of Jesus: A Feminist Theological Interpretation of the New Testament Infancy Narratives* (Crossroad, 1990) and "The Gospel of Luke" in *The Women's Bible Commentary* (Westminster/John Knox Press, 1992).

Introduction

❦

HERSHEL SHANKS

This is a wonderful time for those of us interested in biblical studies. The field is burgeoning. There are more books and journals and articles than one human being can read, let alone absorb. The field is exploding with exciting new ideas and perspectives.

At the same time, in society in general, we are witnessing a transformation of gender roles and gender perspectives unlike anything the world has ever seen since human beings first walked this earth. We are reassessing what it means to be a woman, and I guess also what it means to be a man. Our topic today lies at the intersection of these two exciting and enormously important developments, where gender studies and biblical studies meet.

The Bible is generally considered the most enriching collection of books ever written. For many, it is the word of God, Himself...or Herself...or Itself. You see the problem already. Before the advent of the modern age, the Bible was studied mostly from a theological or literary viewpoint. Modern critical studies have opened up a whole range of new approaches. We want to know when the Bible was written, how it developed, what claims it has to historical accuracy and what the biblical world was like.

The tools of archaeology, sociology, anthropology, linguistics, comparative religion, and all the subdivisions and subdisciplines of each, are being brought to bear in our effort to plumb the depths of this great book. How would an economist look at the financial dealings reflected in the Bible? How would a general assess the military tactics and strategies? How would a political scientist understand the development of government and administrative institutions? It's only natural that with all these new, and old, approaches we would also look at the Bible from the viewpoint of our new understandings of gender, the relations between men and women and their respective roles and attitudes in the biblical world.

In short, how does a modern feminist—and I include in that term men as well as women—look at the text, relate to the text? I don't have to tell you that this is a sensitive subject. We are, after all, dealing with a sacred, holy text. Yet few would dispute that the biblical world was a patriarchal world. How does a feminist look for meaning in a biblical text that is essentially patriarchal?

Scholars have answered that question in a variety of ways, as we will hear from our speakers. They have also asked the question in a variety of ways, and that is, perhaps, more important. How one views the Bible often depends on what questions one asks, not simply on the answers one gives.

For example, we may ask how the Bible stories reflect the concerns of women, how women's interests are treated. We may consider women's roles. We may look at the lives of biblical women from a modern perspective, not just from the purview of the biblical world. We may look for distortions borne of a patriarchal perspective. And we may ask how we, as modern, 20th-century readers, relate to the text. Do these questions deepen our appreciation of the text? Do they lead to new perspectives on the text? Or do they lead us, in some instances, to reject the text?

I must tell you that I find this adventure enormously enriching. Sometimes people find new approaches to the Bible, like the feminist approach, threatening, even destructive. Will they in effect destroy faith? Will they cheapen or show disrespect for the biblical text? For me, it is exactly the opposite. It is not simply that they don't do this, but they are a positive good. They are an affirmative enlightenment, and they offer a deepening understanding.

Some of our childlike understandings of the Bible and the biblical text, I think, may keep us from a full appreciation of the deeper resonances of the text. When we explore the text from a feminist perspective, we understand another layer of the text. We relate to it more sensitively.

We will be exploring questions today, not in an abstract way as I have just been doing, but with close examinations of particular texts and the particular people who walk the pages of those texts—people like Eve, Miriam, Mary Magdalene, and the men with whom they relate. We will be asking challenging questions. How can difficult texts be reclaimed for women? In what special ways is the Bible a spiritual resource for women? Can it always be reclaimed, or are there texts that cannot be considered authoritative from a feminist viewpoint? How has the Bible been used to suppress women?

Our speakers today are astral figures in the field, and you will hear a variety of approaches, not just one. They will not always agree, but these scholars are some of the most insightful, creative biblical scholars working in the area of feminist studies. I know them all personally, and they are, in a sense, my teachers. I am not a scholar. I know how they have inspired and enriched me, and I am sure they will do the same for you.

I can tell you about the standing of our first speaker with a little story. Elie Wiesel gives a series of lectures every year at the 92nd Street "Y" in New York on different biblical figures, and he mentioned to me that he was going to give one lecture this year on Miriam. Of course, that immediately brought up the subject of Phyllis Trible's work.

He told me he didn't know Phyllis, so I suggested luncheon together, and he jumped at the opportunity. I called Phyllis, and the three of us shared a long, leisurely lunch at Le Perigord. It was a wonderful occasion. I just sat there quietly in the middle and listened. I'm only sorry I didn't record the conversation because it was magnificent.

Elie Wiesel and Hershel Shanks are not the only people who hold Phyllis Trible in high regard. The 4,500 members of the prestigious Society of Biblical Literature, all scholars, elected her their current president. She delivered her presidential address to thousands of Bible scholars assembled at the annual meeting of the society in Chicago on November 19, 1994. Phyllis is best known to the general public for her two path-breaking books, God and the Rhetoric of Sexuality and Texts of Terror: Literary Feminist Readings of Biblical Narratives.

It is a pleasure for me to present to you the Baldwin Professor of Sacred Literature at Union Theological Seminary in New York, Professor Phyllis Trible, who will speak on "Eve and Miriam: From the Margins to the Center." —H.S.

Eve and Miriam: From the Margins to the Center

PHYLLIS TRIBLE

In the year of her 80th birthday (1895), the feminist Elizabeth Cady Stanton published *The Woman's Bible*, an effort, as she described it, to "have women's commentaries on women's position in the Old and New Testaments."[1] Stanton worked against formidable odds, most tellingly, opposition from other suffragists who thought their larger cause would suffer if they attacked entrenched religious interests. Women scholars of the time who were versed in biblical criticism and biblical languages refused to help her for fear that an unpopular subject would compromise their reputations and attainments. But Stanton persevered. Her controversial work became a best-seller, though its effect upon scholarship and religious thinking was minimal. For 70 to 80 years thereafter, the feminist task of reinterpreting the Bible lay dormant, as did feminism itself.

In 1963 a midwestern housewife named Betty Friedan published *The Feminine Mystique*, a book destined to alter the scene in North America and throughout the world.[2] Marking the beginning of the second wave of feminism, this book placed on the agenda of the nation the issue of what it means to be female and male. Within a few years (1968), the religious community took on this issue, first through another book entitled *The Church and the Second Sex*. Although the author Mary Daly has since repudiated her own writing because of its reformist rather than revolutionary stance, in its time this work dominated theological debate about gender.[3] Shortly thereafter, women biblical scholars began to engage the debate.

Unlike their 19th-century sisters, they have been willing to risk reputations and attainments. Their growing numbers and scholarly qualifications have compelled a respectful hearing within the academic community. So over the past two decades, a new perspective, perhaps even a new discipline, has emerged: feminist interpretation of the Bible.

A few years after Daly published her book, I left the South and moved to Boston, where Daly was speaking frequently to various groups. I listened attentively to what she had to say, not having to be convinced of feminism, for I knew that it was bone of my bones and flesh of my flesh. But at the same time I knew, decidedly at variance with Daly, that the Bible fed my life in rich and beneficial ways. The Bible that I grew up with in Sunday School, where "sword drills" were routine—I think a few people in this audience know about "sword drills" (Laughter.)—and memorization of biblical verses was mandatory, *that* Bible continued to make a claim upon me. To be sure, I learned in college and later in graduate school that the Bible is rather different from what Sunday School teachers and some preachers tell us. But not even critical and sophisticated ways of studying it supplanted or diminished my love for it. There is power in the document, and it need not work adversely for women or for men. This I knew and this I know, no matter how much others may rush to say it isn't so.

But there was a rub. To know that one is a feminist and to know that one loves the Bible is, in the thinking of many, at best an oxymoron, perhaps clever as a rhetorical statement but surely not a possibility for existential living. After all, if no man can serve two masters, no woman can serve two authorities, a master called Scripture and a mistress called Feminism. And so my predicament grew as I heard the challenge that Daly and others posed and continue to pose. "Choose ye this day whom you will serve, the God of the Fathers or the God of Sisterhood. Biblical religion gives us the God of the Fathers. In it is no resting place for feminists." If this be true, then I am of all women most wretched, or whatever adjective seems fitting: confused, schizophrenic, misguided, conservative, or just plain wrong.

To sketch how this perceived predicament works itself out in my life, let us begin with a statement I have never doubted, with an observation that is overwhelming as description and condemnation. The Bible was born and bred in a land of patriarchy; it abounds in male imagery and language. For centuries, interpreters have explored and exploited this male language to articulate theology, to shape the contours of the church, the synagogue and the academy, and to instruct human beings, male and female, in who they are, what roles they should play, how they should behave. So harmonious has seemed this association of Scripture with sexism, of faith with culture, that few people throughout the ages have even questioned or analyzed it. Understandably, when feminism turns attention to the Bible, it first of all names the document as patriarchal. To name it thus means more than putting a label or tag of identification upon it. It means investigating patriarchy and beyond that indicting the Bible for this sin.

Feminism has no difficulty making a case against the Bible. It has no difficulty convicting the Bible of patriarchy. One could say that this recognition is the sine qua non of all feminist readings of the Bible. And yet the recognition that the Bible is a patriarchal document has led to different conclusions.[4]

Some feminists—they may be secular or religious— denounce the Bible as hopelessly misogynous. It is, they tell us, a woman-hating document, and there is no health in it. Other feminists have reprehensibly used patriarchal data to support anti-Semitic sentiments. They may posit a prehistoric or early historic era of what they think was "good" goddess worship that was undercut, discredited and demolished by the ascendancy of the Hebrew God. Still others may believe that whereas the "Old Testament" is terribly bad on this issue the New Testament brings an improved revelation. (I suggest that whoever thinks that should read the New Testament some time.) (Chuckles.) Still

other feminists read the Bible as an historical document, devoid
of any continuing authority and hence worthy of dismissal.

So from time to time the question comes, who cares? But
if we are attuned to the world, the church and the synagogue,
we know that a lot of people care. They enlist the Bible repeat-
edly in support of their political and social agendas. I need not
say more about that in this setting and in this city. (Chuckles.)
Thus some feminists succumb to despair about the ever-
present male power that the Bible and its commentators hold
over women. And still others, unwilling to let the case against
women be the determining word, insist that the text and its
interpreters provide more excellent ways.

This last approach is my niche. How did I get here? First,
with the recognition that the Bible is a patriarchal text. Second,
with the conviction, indeed the realization, that the Bible can
be redeemed from bondage to patriarchy; that redemption is
already at work in the text; and that the articulation of it is
desirable and beneficial. Sometimes it is even fun. To bring
together the self-critique that operates in the Bible with the
concerns of feminism is to shape an interpretation that makes
a difference for all of us—an interpretation that begins with suspicion and becomes subversion, but subversion for the sake of
redemption, for the sake of healing, wholeness and well-being.

What are the elements of this approach? Reinterpreting
familiar texts is one procedure. Reinterpretation does not
mean making the Bible say whatever the reader wants it to say.
It does not hold that there are no limits to interpretation and
that the text can, in effect, be rewritten. But reinterpretation
does recognize the polyvalency of the text: that any text is open
to multiple interpretations, that between those who adamantly
hold fast to only one meaning and those who breezily claim
that the text can be manipulated to say anything is a wide spec-
trum of legitimate meanings. Some of these meanings assert
themselves boldly, and others have to be teased out.

Reinterpretation also recognizes the diversity of Scripture. The Bible is not a single-minded document; rather it teems with diverse voices and points of view. Despite attempts to harmonize it, by ancient redactors working within it for canonization or by modern commentators working from the outside to establish and reestablish its authority, the Bible itself comes to us full of struggles, battles, contradictions and problems. It refuses to be the captive of any one group or perspective.

Fittingly then, if ironically, even the winners who prevail in Scripture—those whose points of view tried to stamp out other points of view—bear witness to the stories of the losers. And in the very process of trying to discredit these stories, the winners gave them canonical status. Understanding that every culture contains a counterculture, feminism seeks those other voices in the Bible. It is open to exploiting diversity and plurality.

Further, reinterpretation emphasizes the pilgrim character of the Bible. It knows that all Scripture is a pilgrim wandering through history, engaging in new settings, and ever-refusing to be locked in the box of the past. Every generation or group that engages the text comes to it from certain perspectives not adopted by others, with certain questions not asked by others, and with certain issues not raised by others. One group sees what another does not, at the same time acknowledging that we all see in part, not in whole. So this pilgrim book has maintained a lively dialogue with generations of readers, for weal and for woe.

To illustrate reinterpretation, let us return to the most familiar of all texts, the story of the Garden of Eden in Genesis 2–3. We hardly need reminding that throughout the ages this text has been used to legitimate patriarchy as the will of God. So powerful has been the patriarchal interpretation that it has burrowed its way into the collective psyche of the Western world. We think we know what the text says, and we think it tells us that man was created first and woman last— and that the order of creation is a value judgment making her subordinate to him. She is his derivative, having come from his side. She is described as his "helper"; surely that means his assistant, not his equal. She seduces him and so is blamed for their disobedience. And we are told that she is cursed. She is punished by being subjected to the rule of her husband.

Now if this be your exegesis of the text, be clear that your understanding is no different from any patriarchal reading proposed by men throughout the ages. The difference may come in evaluation, in deciding whether or not this story is to hold power over your life. Given this particular interpretation, the choice is clear for the feminist. She denounces the story; she rejects it, a response with which we are all familiar.

But that is not the response of *this* feminist, as you no doubt may have guessed. Long ago I asked myself this question—how come, if, as it certainly appears, this story is so terribly patriarchal, how come I like it? How come it feeds and nourishes my life? How come I feel no anger in reading this story, no embarrassment in proclaiming it? How come it gives me a sense of well-being despite its tragic ending? In pondering these questions, I thought there had to be another interpretation at work in the text. How else could I explain the way the story draws me unto itself? Over time, fragments of thought began to surface in my mind. I shall tell you two of them.

I remembered a Southern Baptist missionary who, having returned from foreign lands, was given the assignment of teaching little girls in summer camp. I was one of those little girls. We belonged to a group called the G.A.'s. (As some of you know, that group is still with us today.) In Southern Baptist churches there were groups for boys and groups for girls. The boys were called R.A.'s, the girls G.A.'s. G.A.'s meant Girls Auxiliary.[5] R.A.'s meant Royal Ambassadors. (Laughter.)

So in summer camp it did not matter too much who taught the G.A.'s. "We will put the little girls off to the side, and we will ask this woman missionary to take care of them for Bible study." Well, that's when subversion happens. (Laughter.)

This woman said to us, "Little girls, everything that God created got better and better. What was the last thing God created?" (Laughter, Applause.) Now in unison and with great vigor, we replied, "Man." And she said, "No. Woman." Hers is not the precise interpretation with which I have ended up. (Chuckles.) But nonetheless, to this day, I am grateful for her word. It resonated deeply within me, though at the time I knew it not.

Many years passed, and one day I was sitting in a classroom at Union Theological Seminary in New York. The course was entitled Old Testament Theology. The professor was a learned scholar whom no one would ever accuse of being a feminist. (Chuckles.) Carefully, in great detail, he analyzed the story of the Garden. All that he said I fervently recorded in my notes, and then in the years that followed I rarely, if ever, consulted those notes...until that day came, that day when another fragment of thought surfaced in my mind, and I sought out those notes. I found what I vaguely remembered. The professor said something like this. The portrayal of the man in the Garden in Genesis 2–3 is not the portrayal of a patriarch. Whereas the woman is depicted as alert, intelligent and sensitive, the man comes off as passive, bland and belly-oriented. All he can do is eat. (Chuckles.)

Surely enough, as I reread the text, I saw that the woman, before she eats, contemplates the tree. She finds it good to eat; that is, it has a physical appeal. She finds it pleasant to see; it has an aesthetic dimension. She finds it desirable for wisdom, a sapiential motif. The story that moves so rapidly pauses at this point to let us watch the woman as she contemplates, her vision encompassing the gamut of life. Only then does she eat.

By contrast, the man "who was with her"—now that in itself is a telling phrase, and until recently it was deleted in most Bible translations. If you look up the reasons for deleting it, you will find people saying we don't need it. But excising it has led to all kinds of erroneous interpretations. The text says quite clearly, "the man who was with her." It's in every Hebrew manuscript; it's in the Septuagint, the Greek translation. If you are interested in the history of translations, I found it lacking in Jerome's Vulgate. (Laughter.) But the man who was with her didn't contemplate. He ate.

How grateful I am, and shall always be, for this insight from the lips of the professor. He knew not what he was doing that day. (Chuckles.) But at some deep level, his exegesis resonated with feminist flesh and bone. These and other fragments of thought that surfaced after years of lying dormant helped me to reread Genesis 2–3 from a feminist perspective: to reinterpret it in a way that runs counter to tradition in seeing the text not as legitimation but as critique of patriarchy. Let me recite some of the details of this reinterpretation:[6]

For most people, the story of the Garden begins with the creation of man. All translations would like for us to think that, too. But in Hebrew the story begins in a much more interesting and subtle way. It begins with a wonderful pun, the creation of *hā-ʾādām* from *hā-ʾādāmāh*. You can hear in the pronunciation of the Hebrew the similarities of those words. We have a play on their sounds. Moreover, we are not talking about an individual creature, but *the* (*hā-*), the creature who comes from the soil. It is difficult, as you know, to transfer the puns of one language into another, but in this case I think we can do it. Let us translate, God "formed the human from the humus." As soon as we do that, we have radically altered the interpretation of this text. The point of the first creation is not gender and sexuality but the creation of a creature that comes from the earth, a creature not specifically identified sexually. So the first creature is not male; the first creature is not the first man.

Indeed man, the male, enters this story of creation only with the advent of woman, the female, and that does not happen at the beginning. It happens at the end of chapter 2, where the one earth creature, the one human from the humus, is, through divine surgery, made into two beings, one female and the other male. And interestingly, if the order of words is important to you, the word "female" occurs before the word "male." The two creatures that come from the one earth creature constitute the advent of sexuality in creation. They are bone of bones and flesh of flesh, phrases that mean mutuality and equality. So the first woman, who later receives the name Eve in a strange and ironic way, is not created second to the primal man.

Moreover, she is not created as his helper, that is to say, his assistant and his inferior. To be sure the Hebrew word ʿezer has traditionally been translated "helper," but the translation is totally misleading. If you look the word up in a concordance, you discover that most often in the Hebrew Bible it is used to describe God. God is the helper of Israel. And when we hear that God is the helper of Israel, we never think that God is inferior to Israel. To the contrary, we know God is superior to Israel. God is the one who creates and saves Israel.

So then, if we have trouble with this word as applied to the woman, it is not the trouble we thought we had. The connotations of the word are connotations of superiority. I think the storyteller recognizes the issue because the storyteller does not allow the word to stand alone but adds to it another word: an ʿezer, "fit for," an ʿezer, "corresponding to." The point is to temper the connotation of superiority.

The woman Eve is no opposite sex, no second sex, no derived sex. She is not Adam's rib. Indeed that "rib," or perhaps that "side," which belongs anyway not to the man but to the sexually undifferentiated first creature, is but the raw material for divine activity. God takes that raw material and "builds" it into woman. Most translations say "makes" it, which is a tamer verb. But the Hebrew verb *banah* indicates considerable labor to produce solid and lasting results. It's a word used for building towers, cities and fortifications.

The primal woman is no weak, dainty, ephemeral creature. Indeed, she is the culmination of the story, fulfilling humanity in sexuality. Though equal in creation with the man, she is actually elevated in the design of the story. Therefore, "a man leaves his father and his mother, and cleaves to his woman, and they become one flesh" (Genesis 2:24). That is hardly the pattern of patriarchal culture. And interestingly enough, the man alone is identified with parents. The woman stands alone; her independence as a human creature remains intact. To her the man comes. He does not control her; rather, he moves towards her for union. In her very creation, this woman shatters traditional ideas that have clustered around her.

And she does something more. She engages in the world's first conversation, mythically speaking—a conversation between the serpent and herself. If you were to initiate conversation in the world, what topic would you choose? Why, there's only one—theology, that is to say, God-talk. Even the serpent knows that. So the serpent addresses the woman in Hebrew with plural verb forms. In the South we would say, "Did y'all...Did God say, 'y'all shouldn't eat of that fruit?' " (Genesis 3:1). The serpent recognizes the woman as the spokesperson for the human couple, once again hardly the pattern of patriarchy.

The woman discusses theology with great intelligence, indeed wisdom. When she answers the serpent's question, she states the case for obedience to God even more strongly than God had stated it. She says, "From the fruit of the tree that is in the midst of the Garden, God said, 'You shall not eat from it and you shall not touch it, lest you die'" (Genesis 3:3). Now God had not said anything about touching it. She has added the phrase, "you shall not *touch* it," and thereby her interpretive skills begin to emerge.

Not only can the woman relay the command of God, but she can interpret it faithfully. Her understanding guarantees obedience. If the tree is not touched, its fruit cannot be eaten. As I pondered her words some time ago, I thought that here Eve is building what the rabbis called "a fence around Torah." They created additional laws to protect the laws of God. If you obey the laws that they put like a fence around the sacred laws, you will never disobey God. And that is exactly what she is doing. If we cannot touch the fruit, then we will never eat it.

Eve, the first rabbi? (Chuckles.) I wondered what rabbinic commentaries might say about that. One day, a friend and I checked. We read a sentence something like this: "Here, indeed, the woman builds a fence around Torah; *Adam told her what to do.*" (Laughter.) *I tell you that he did not.* (Laughter.) She was the one who spoke with clarity and authority. Eve is theologian, ethicist, hermeneut (that is, interpreter), preacher and rabbi. She defies the stereotypes of patriarchal culture, and she provides us with a powerful statement about the creation of the female. It is not the statement that the church, the academy and the synagogue have traditionally made about women.

Now if the structural, verbal and grammatical ambiguities of this ancient story yield interpretations that defy patriarchy and open up other possibilities for interpreting the story and for appropriating it in new ways, the text thereby encourages us to look even further within the Bible, to listen for other accents and other voices that subvert patriarchy.

That encouragement brings me to a second female, the woman Miriam. I first became interested in her because of my interest in the issue of authority, an issue I think feminism has posed to the biblical text and to the faith of Christians and Jews in a way that has never been done before. I asked myself who in Scripture posed the question of authority. As far as I could remember, the first was none other than Miriam. She wanted to know whether God spoke only through Moses. "Does God not also speak through Aaron and me?" she asked (Numbers 12:2).

Miriam's story begins long before she asks this question. It begins when she, as the unnamed sister of Moses, plays a mediating role in saving her baby brother at the River Nile (Exodus 2:1-10). She and other women play prominent roles at the beginning of the Exodus event. But once the Exodus event gets underway, what happens to these women? Why, they disappear. They get submerged in the text—not in the sea, but in the text. And Moses, Pharaoh and God begin to struggle through the plagues and the sea crossing. The men eclipse the women.

As the narrative reaches the sea, Moses takes center stage. He stretches out his hand; the sea recedes. He stretches out his hand; the sea returns. Israel walks on dry ground; the Egyptians lie dead upon the shore (Exodus 14:21–31). "When the strife is o'er and the battle done," Israel celebrates the victory won. A magnificent song appears on the lips of Moses and the men of Israel (Exodus 15:1–18). The first of many stanzas sets the tone and the content:

> I will sing to the Lord
> who has triumphed gloriously.
> Horse and rider God has thrown
> into the sea.

Literarily and theologically, this long litany of triumph climaxes and closes the Exodus story. Accordingly, readers of the text who pay attention to how literature takes shape, expect the story to move on to another topic, to move into the wilderness narrative. But that does not happen.

Instead, what follows the grand hymnic conclusion is a small section that recapitulates the event at the sea, thereby returning to all the struggles that preceded closure. That's a jarring way to organize a text. It seems awkward, repetitious and misplaced. An attentive reader with feminist sensibilities begins to suspect tampering with the text. As she reads on, the suspicion intensifies. We find these words: "Then Miriam the prophet, the sister of Aaron, took timbrel in her hands, and all the women went out after her with timbrels and dances, and Miriam answered them, 'Sing to the Lord most glorious deity, horse and rider God has hurled into the sea'" (Exodus 15:20–21). These words from Miriam match the first stanza of the hymn attributed to Moses. But only after her words do we get closure to the Exodus and then move into the

wilderness. I suggest that we ponder this arrangement, especially asking what it means that this little story about Miriam
and the women was preserved.

The story reads on the surface as if Miriam repeated the first
stanza of the long poem assigned to Moses. Not only did she not
sing the entire song (just the first verse), but she didn't get it
exactly right. She changed it. So people may conclude that, by
comparison, her performance is deficient. Back in the 1950s,
however, long before there was feminist interpretation of the
Bible, two male scholars (both of whom write for *Bible Review*),
wrote an article on the so-called Song of Moses, or the Song of
the Sea, in which they argued that the very fact the little Miriamic
ending is preserved is a clue that in an earlier stage of the tradition
the entire song belonged to Miriam and the women of Israel, not
to Moses.[7] In this connection, recall the ancient songs explicitly
attributed to women, the Song of Deborah and the Song of
Hannah. Now add the Song of Miriam.

But what did tradition do? Tradition, eager to elevate
Moses, took the song right out of the mouth of Miriam and
gave it to him. And remember, he was supposed to be inartic-
ulate (Exodus 4:10–17). By such a procedure redactors both
preserved and destroyed the women's story. They kept Miriam,
giving her the first stanza, but they diminished her importance.
What does feminist interpretation do? It looks at these marginal
voices. It looks at these people in the shadows, and it brings
them forth.[8]

So then, like the beginning, the end of the Exodus belongs
to women. The central woman is Miriam. We meet her first at
the bank of the River Nile. Next we see her at the shore of the
sea. She is a mediator who has become a percussionist, lyricist,
vocalist, prophet, leader and theologian. This hidden Miriam
tells a different version of the Exodus story from the visible
Moses. Her voice is worth hearing. But you say to me, "Don't
stop there because the next time we hear about her, she poses
the question of authority that gets her into trouble, 'Does the

Lord speak only through Moses? Does the Lord not also speak through Aaron and me?' (Numbers 12:2). Miriam was reprimanded severely for asking that question."

God answered her question and made it quite clear that Moses stands peerless at the top in the prophetic order. Further, God zapped Miriam and Aaron with some kind of punishment. But the punishment was not equal. Miriam got the worst of it. Translated literally, the text says, "The nostril of the Lord burned against them and God left" (Numbers 12:9). God glorified Moses with the divine mouth. With the divine nose, God attacked Aaron and Miriam. This divinity is made of stern stuff.

Now when the divine glory and anger depart, we behold Miriam alone stricken with scales like snow (Numbers 12:10). Red hot anger has become a cold white disease. A scaring emotion produces a scarred body. The Exodus in which Miriam has led in such a triumphal way brings us to a repudiation of her. But Aaron beseeches Moses on her behalf, so that, in time, she is restored to the community of Israel (Numbers 12:11–16). Yet we do not hear any more about her for several chapters. Never does she speak again, and never does she have a major role in the wilderness experiences of the people. It is as though a vendetta has been launched against her, and that vendetta continues unto her death.

Silences and juxtapositions unfold the tale. Just preceding the obituary for Miriam comes a lengthy section of ritual prescriptions (Numbers 19). In content as well as in placement, they work to indict Miriam. The first prescription concerns preparing special water for impurity. To the burning of a cow the priest will add cedar wood, hyssop and scarlet yarn. Though the text does not specify the meaning of these ingredients, we know from Leviticus (14:1–9) that they are used in the cleansing of one with a diseased skin, truly a reminder of Miriam's punishment. At the appropriate time, running water is added to the mixture, and its use awaits a second prescription that pertains to those who become unclean through contact with the dead.

Seven days are required for their purification, the same time needed for the cleansing of diseased skin.

Immediately following these two prescriptions, the one alluding to diseased skin and the other emphasizing the uncleanliness of the dead, comes the announcement of Miriam's death. "And the people of Israel, the whole community, came into the Wilderness of Zin in the first month, and the people stayed in Kadesh. And Miriam died and was buried there" (Numbers 20:1). She never spoke again. If we accept only the surface level of the text, this is the ending the Bible gives to this uppity woman.

But I don't accept only surface meanings. I try to tease out of the text the hidden stories, the stories of the losers. In doing that, I isolate six fragments that disclose a different version of the Miriamic story.

The first fragment comes in the reaction of the people at the time Miriam is punished by God. God sends word, after the episode about authority, that the people are to move on. They are to continue the journey. But what do we read? The people refuse to do that until Miriam is restored to them (Numbers 12:15). God may tell them to move on, Moses may tell them to move on, but they do not set out on the march until Miriam is brought in again. They wait for her. Those whom she served do not forsake her in her time of tribulation. This steadfast devotion of the people to Miriam indicates a story different from the regnant one.

The second fragment brings us to the symbol of water, a symbol that supports Miriam in interesting ways. The first time we see her, she is by the River Nile. The next time we see her is at the triumphal crossing of the sea. No life-giving waters emerge, however, when in the wilderness authorities conspire to punish her. Diseased flesh bespeaks arid land. In the ritual prescriptions preceding her obituary, the symbol of water appears with ambivalence. The water for impurity mediates between cleanliness and uncleanliness. Miriam dies, thereby becoming unclean. Yet at her death, no water for impurity is invoked. Instead, a striking thing happens, though translations do not encourage us to recognize it.

They report Miriam's obituary, put a period, and then begin a new paragraph. Sometimes they even put a space between the obituary and the new paragraph, thereby suggesting that we are not to make any connection between the two sentences.[9] But when we do connect them, we learn something important: "In Kadesh, Miriam died and was buried there. Now there was no water for the community" (Numbers 20:1–2). Nature is responding to Miriam's death. The response is immediate and severe. Nature mourns; the wells in the desert dry up. Miriam, protector of her brother at the riverbank and leader in victory at the sea, symbolized life. How appropriate then that the waters of life should reverence her death. Like the people of Israel, nature honors Miriam.

A third fragment: After her burial, the lack of water introduces a long narrative critical of Moses and Aaron (Numbers 20). In structure, it balances the prescriptions preceding her death announcement. In effect, it counters the vendetta against her. Once again, the people attack their leaders, Moses and Aaron, because of overwhelming miseries. The two men appeal to God, who instructs them to secure water from a rock. They are successful, but God is displeased and decrees that neither man shall lead the people into the land. Miriam's death has initiated their demise. Soon thereafter, when the congregation has sojourned from Kadesh to Mount Horeb, Aaron dies, and in time Moses follows. If Miriam never reached the Promised Land, neither did her brothers.

After the death of Miriam, the wells in the desert dry up, the people rebel again, God censures Moses and Aaron, Aaron dies, and the days of Moses are numbered. However much the detractors of Miriam have tried, they do not control the story. There are more interpretations than are dreamt of in their hermeneutics.

Beyond the Exodus and wilderness accounts, a fourth fragment of a pro-Miriamic tradition surfaced in the Hebrew Scriptures. If certain groups repudiated Miriam forever, the prophets reclaimed her. In fact, they stated boldly what others worked hard to deny, namely, that in early Israel Miriam belonged to a triad of leaders. She was the equal of Moses and Aaron. In Micah 6:4, God speaks, "For I brought you up from the land of Egypt, I redeemed you from the house of bondage, and I sent before you Moses, Aaron and Miriam." Here prophecy acknowledges the full legitimacy of Miriam, its own ancestor, who was designated "the prophet" even before her brother Moses received the title (cf. Deuteronomy 18:15). If you are bothered by the fact that in this list her name comes last, and you think that order suggests a lowly position for her, let me counter with a well-known biblical truth: "The first shall be last, and the last first" (cf. Matthew 19:30).

A fifth fragment shows Miriam animating the musical life of Israel. If Jubal be its mythical father (Genesis 4:21), she is its historical mother. She inaugurates a procession of women who move throughout Scripture singing and dancing in sorrow and in joy. Think of the daughter of Jephthah in the days of the judges, who comes out to meet her father with timbrels and dances (Judges 11:3–4). Later the virgin daughters of Shiloh come out to dance in the dances (Judges 21:21). And in the days of the monarchy, when warriors returned victorious from battle, the women come out of all the cities singing and dancing with timbrels, songs of joy and instruments of music (1 Samuel 18:6–7). All these women with timbrels and dances are heirs of Miriam.

From these narrative texts, her musical legacy passes into liturgical tradition. Read the psalms, and you will hear resonances of Miriam. A psalmist describes a parade entering the temple, with the singers in front, the minstrels last, and between them the women playing timbrels (Psalms 68:24–25). Another psalm based on Exodus and wilderness memories echoes

Miriam, "Raise a song," it says, "sound the timbrel" (Psalms 149:3–4). Similarly, a third proclaims, "Let Israel praise God's name with dancing, making melody with timbrel and lyre" (Psalms 149:3). And in the grand finale of the Psalter, where everything that breathes is called upon to praise God, the woman Miriam breathes in the last line, "Praise the Lord with timbrel and dance" (Psalm 150:4).

For a sixth fragment, let us move beyond the Hebrew Scriptures as indeed the story of Miriam moves beyond them. Though we might move into Jewish midrash or into the Gnostic gospels, I chose to move into the Second Testament. My clue is the Greek name Mary, which is the equivalent of the Hebrew name Miriam. Once you understand that, then you find Miriam resurfacing in the Gospel narratives after centuries of silence. A multitude of Marys attests to the enduring life of Miriam.

As the first Miriam chanted a litany of triumph to the women at the sea, so Mary, pregnant with the child Jesus, sings a song of exaltation (the Magnificat) in response to a blessing from Elizabeth (Luke 1:39–56). We all know that the Song of Hannah (1 Samuel 2) provides vocabulary and themes for the Magnificat, but few of us know that the Song of the Sea, the Song of Miriam (Exodus 15), does the same.

Listen, for example, to these lines juxtaposed from the two songs (SS=Song of the Sea; M=Magnificat):

SS: I will sing to the Lord, most glorious deity.
M: My spirit rejoices in God my Saviour.

SS: Thy right hand, O Lord, glorious in power;
    thy right hand, O Lord, shatters the enemy.
M: God has shown strength with the divine arm,
    has scattered the proud in the imaginations of
    their hearts.

SS: Pharaoh's chariots and his hosts God hurled into the sea.
M: God has put down the mighty from their thrones.

In assigning the name Mary to the mother of the Messiah, Christian tradition honors Miriam, the mother of deliverance. From the birth of Moses to the birth of Israel to the birth of the Messiah, Miriam now enters the ministry of Jesus. In Mary of Bethany the prophet of the Exodus becomes the disciple who chooses the better portion (Luke 10:38–42). On another occasion, when she anoints the feet of Jesus and wipes them with her hair, he defends her action against criticism (Luke 7:36–50; John 12:1–7) and thereafter emulates it himself by washing the feet of the disciples (John 13:3–11). Mary, that is to say Miriam, sets the ritual that Jesus follows, a ritual that subverts established meanings and proper procedures. In such actions she reflects her namesake.

Again, Miriam, healed of leprosy, re-emerges in Mary called Magdalene from whom seven demons have gone out. In a composite picture, this Mary figures prominently at the crucifixion and resurrection. She stands at the cross of Jesus, witnesses his entombment, brings spices for anointing the body, discovers the empty tomb, hears the angelic announcement, sees and talks to the risen Lord (see Matthew 27:57–61; 28:1–10; Mark 16:1–8; Luke 24:10; John 20:1–18). Above all, Mary Magdalene, this Miriam, joined by other women, is the first individual to proclaim the resurrection (Luke 24:10).

All the Marys who witness crucifixion embody in name and deed Miriam, who herself was crucified in the power struggles of the wilderness. All the Marys who proclaim the resurrection, only to hear disbelieving men say they speak an idle tale, incarnate Miriam, whose good news male authorities also demeaned. But in the surprising, indeed subversive, turns of faith, the male judgments did not prevail. "O foolish men," says the text, "and slow of heart to believe all that the prophets have spoken" (Luke 24:25). The Marys got it right. They are Miriam *rediviva*, the woman who first challenged authority.

To lift up Miriam and to lift up Eve, to discern their stories from the margins, is to begin the redemption of Scripture from the confines of patriarchy. To this task feminists who love the Bible have dedicated themselves. In reading Scripture, they exploit its ambiguities and complexities, and they see it as setting before all of us life and death, blessing and curse, liberation and patriarchy. Then they hear the word of God coming from the ancient world to the present, "Choose life, that you and your descendants may live" (Deuteronomy 30:19).

E N D N O T E S

1. Elizabeth Cady Stanton, *The Woman's Bible* (New York: European Publishing Company, 1895–1898), p. 9.

2. Betty Friedan, *The Feminine Mystique* (New York: W.W. Norton & Company, Inc., 1963).

3. Mary Daly, *The Church and the Second Sex* (New York: Harper & Row, 1968; with a new, feminist post-Christian introduction, 1975).

4. On these conclusions, cf., e.g., Susannah Heschel, "Anti-Judaism in Christian Feminist Theology," *Tikkun* (May/June 1990), pp. 25–28, 95–97; for a balanced discussion of goddesses and biblical religion, see Tikva Frymer-Kensky, *In the Wake of the Goddesses: Women, Culture, and the Biblical Transformation of Pagan Myth* (New York: Macmillan, Free Press, 1992).

5. I am told that these letters have since been assigned the meaning "Girls in Action." The change makes no difference as long as boys continue to be designated "Royal Ambassadors."

6. For the full examination of this text, see Phyllis Trible, *God and the Rhetoric of Sexuality* (Philadelphia: Fortress Press, 1978), pp. 72–143.

7. Frank Moore Cross, Jr., and David Noel Freedman, "The Song of Miriam," *Journal of Near Eastern Studies* 14 (1955), pp. 237–250.

8. For a full discussion, see Trible, "Bringing Miriam Out of the Shadows," *Bible Review* 5:1 (1989), pp. 14–25, 34.

9. Cf., e.g., the RSV, NRSV, NJV and NAB.

Tikva Frymer-Kensky is a wonderful human being whom I've known for a long time. She observes the Sabbath, she does not drive on the Sabbath, which begins Friday night. So last night we all went to the hotel where our speakers are staying, to eat. Before we went to the restaurant, we met in Tikva's room and said the Sabbath blessings, including the chanting of the Kiddush, the traditional blessing over the Sabbath meal. And I think we were all taken aback at what a gorgeous, beautiful voice Tikva has. In some ways, I wish this were a concert today, instead of a lecture.

On the other hand, Tikva is one of the sharpest and broadest Bible scholars it has ever been my privilege to meet and interact with. She received her Ph.D. from Yale. She has taught at the University of Michigan, Wayne State, Beer-sheva University in Israel and the Jewish Theological Seminary in New York. She is currently director of biblical studies at the Reconstructionist Rabbinical College in Philadelphia. This January she will be going to Chicago as a full professor in the Divinity School at the University of Chicago. We congratulate her and wish her well in her prestigious new position as professor of Hebrew Bible.

Tikva is the author of several books, including The Judicial Ordeal in the Ancient Near East. *She is, incidentally, also a legal historian. She has another book about to be published,* Mother Prayer, *and, most relevant to her talk today, her most recent book,* In the Wake of the Goddesses. *She will address us today on "Goddesses: Biblical Echoes." —H.S.*

Goddesses: Biblical Echoes

❧

TIKVA FRYMER-KENSKY

The current interest in women in the Bible is partly theological. The wave of feminism has raised fundamental questions about the nature of monotheism, the sexuality of monotheism and the gender messages it conveys. In the last 25 years or so, a new mythology has grown, the mythology of *the* Goddess, the Great Goddess, who was peaceful, earth-loving, women-loving, everything of perfection that can be imagined, and who was displaced by patriarchy.

This is a myth that is growing into a new religion. It has no relationship to historical fact, but it has become a foundational document and an orientational theology for many women struggling with the issues of how to maintain a religious consciousness when that consciousness has, for so long, been accompanied by cultural messages of unequal gender relationships and male domination in a hierarchy.

When we look at history, we realize that the myth of the Great Goddess is less history than psychology because, to some extent, it represents the wish of all of us to go back to the absolute peace and bliss we felt at our mother's breast and even before that in our mother's womb. The real world is not that peaceful; the real world is certainly not that blissful.

The last 150 years have witnessed not only the development of many historical techniques for studying the Bible, but also the development of the great disciplines of history and archaeology. We have discovered the ancient civilizations that surrounded and accompanied Israel, sometimes with animosity and sometimes with cultural interchange, on Israel's quest for a religious conception of the world. These are the cultures of ancient Mesopotamia, Egypt, Canaan, the Hittites, the Edomites, the Moabites and, to a lesser extent, the Greeks.

We know those languages now, more or less—our Edomite is a bit shaky, our Sumerian is still a little primitive—but we have their documents, particularly of the Mesopotamians, because they had no wood, so they wrote on clay, which is not biodegradable. These documents present us with a picture of living polytheism. What does a priest believe when he stands up and sings a hymn? What does the hymn say, not as recollected hundreds of years later by antiquarians, but in the lived experiences of, at least, elite worshipers?

When we read these documents, we realize that some of our precious new myths of this halcyon antiquity are not borne out by the facts. I'll mention just one, the one that is repeated so often in biblical studies—that the Canaanites had a female-centered, earth-friendly religion. When we read the texts, we find that the three female figures in Canaanite texts are extremely marginal and that the world is seen as a competition between the male forces of El, Baal, Mut and Yah.

I like to focus on Sumer because there we have the most texts—a third-millennium assemblage of texts, extending into the first several hundred years of the second millennium. The second millennium—actually the years between 1800 and 1000 B.C.E.—was a time of tremendous transformation. Political institutions became more and more broad scaled. Religion was transformed in a way that continually and constantly diminished the role of goddesses.

The Sumerians invented writing. Their texts show us the most balanced position of female and male deities in the ancient world. But even in Sumerian culture, where our documents start around 2800 B.C.E. with the rudimentary beginnings of writing and end around 1700 B.C.E. with religious texts, we see tremendous changes. We can, in fact, detect a pattern. Female deities are more important early in the Sumerian period and less important later. Female deities that had control over certain cultural events and activities in the early period, let's say in 2300 B.C.E., become sidekicks by the later period.

Nevertheless, let me give you a picture of the role of goddesses in the classic flowering of Sumerian civilization, which is reflected in the literature composed during the periods we call Ur III and the early Old Babylonian period, from about 2200 to 1700 B.C.E. In these texts, goddesses fulfill certain specific functions. They are women in the sky, but they play the same roles in the family as women on earth. Their position and their nature are frequently discussed through stories about family relations.

We have the mother, the sister, the mother-in-law, the daughter (less important) and the wife. The mother is wonderful. There is no dark side to the mother in Mesopotamian mythology. This is long before Sigmund Freud and Melanie Klein. (Chuckles.) The mother is a pasteboard figure who is selfless, devoted and loyal to her child. She does "what's good for you." The sister is her shadow, the most loyal person a man can expect, faithful unto, and even beyond, death. To have a sister is to be the most fortunate of all heroes. Even the mother-in-law is a lovely figure. She is particularly the friend of the daughter-in-law, if you can imagine such a thing. She is her key ally in the house. So that's all the good parts.

What a wife is like we do not know. We do have wives—we have the prototype of all wives, a goddess named Uttu, the goddess of weaving and spinning. In the magic literature, you call upon Uttu when you want to weave a web around someone. You would want to do that because one of the most dramatic kinds of magic ritual involves tying a person up, spinning a spell, and then cutting the threads. As the threads are cut, so are the evil forces that hold this person in their thrall. So Uttu appears fairly regularly in magic literature.

She also appears in several myths, and that's where we realize she is the archetypical wife, just as spinning and weaving are the archetypical wifely duties. Uttu appears first in a tale about the birth of the gods. At first, there are only two divine beings worth mentioning—Enki, a male figure, and Ninhursag, Mother Earth. And they copulate. From this union is born a goddess. Then Enki, who is male water (the subterranean waters and the river waters), copulates with his daughter, and another goddess is born. Enki looks at the new goddess and sees she's beautiful and sleeps with her, too. In each case, he seduces her very easily, and she gives birth very easily, in nine days rather than nine months. And the baby comes out slick as juniper oil.

The fifth or sixth generation is Uttu. When she is born, Ninhursag, the grandmother of all, says to her, "When Enki comes to lie with you, do not say yes. Tell him if he wants you, he must bring you presents." Uttu is a comely female, and Enki desires her. At her request, he performs the Sumerian marriage ceremony—he brings a basket of fruit and knocks on her door. They are married, and they have sex. But Uttu's nine months are not nine days. She has become a wife and has such difficulty giving birth that the mother of all has to turn into the birth goddess—and that is why women always need help.

Uttu appears in another myth important for biblical studies, the story of the ewe lamb and the stalk of wheat. As one kind of entertainment in pre-MTV days, the Mesopotamian elite held banquets where they staged debates between winter and summer—which is more beneficial for humankind—or between the palm and the tamarisk—which is a more important cultural element.

We have some 20-odd debates like this, among which is a debate between a ewe lamb and a stalk of wheat or grain. It begins, as they all do, with how these elements came to be, going back to the beginning. It tells the story of how the gods, when they created humanity, which, as everybody knows, was done for the purpose of providing servants, gave humans the task of feeding them.

But in the beginning humans didn't have very much. When we were first created, we walked around naked like the animals, we ate fruits and grasses, and we drank water. And that's what we gave the gods—because that's what we had. But the gods got sick and tired of drinking water and eating grasses, so they held a council meeting and decided to elevate the condition of humankind so we would have better gifts to give them. (Chuckles.) In order to do that, they created the ewe lamb, the source of wool, and the stalk of grain, the source of bread and beer. They created Uttu, the goddess of spinning and weaving, to teach humans how to make cloth from the ewe lamb. The debate about the ewe lamb and the stalk of wheat then goes off in areas that don't particularly interest us about which is more essential to civilization.

In this myth, Uttu is the foundational, transformative agent that moves us from the realm of natural existence— nakedness, water and grasses—to the beginnings of culture— wearing clothes and bringing meat and bread for the gods. Beyond this we know nothing about Uttu, and that is very significant, not because the texts are haphazardly silent about her, but because what a woman is *supposed* to do, what a wife is *supposed* to do, once she is married, is make cloth, bake bread and make beer. And that's a full-time occupation. Beyond that, she has no persona, no characteristics, no desires, no influence, no life. So the literature tells us nothing about her.

There are two more goddesses I would like to tell you about. Although Uttu, the standard middle-class and poorer-class wife, is not heard from again, upper-class women who are courted by rich men are promised a share of power. In fact, Sumerian royal women exercised considerable administrative duties and diplomatic functions and had a good deal of economic impact.

The image of the upper-class woman is the goddess Ninlil, who is raised like a proper daughter and to whom the god Enlil speaks. Enlil is the chief god of the capital city; he is the essence of the young, macho male who goes to war and then organizes things to his desires.

There are two tales about the meeting of Enlil and Ninlil. In one, he rapes her, is brought to trial and is banished. She, having been thoroughly seduced by the rape (that's a very old myth), follows him to the depths of the netherworld. Enough said about that myth. (Laughter.)

In the other myth, he sees her playing in front of her mother's house. He speaks to her mother and offers his hand in marriage. He promises her that her daughter will become, by marrying him, the chief administrator in Nippur, that she, second only to him, will make decisions and, along with him, decide the fates—kind of like Rosalynn and Hillary. (Chuckles.) In both the rape version and the marriage version of the tale, Ninlil becomes the mother of a vast array of important gods, all of whom are related to Enlil. She is the queen and queen mother who shares her husband's reflected glory and position.

The most enduring goddess, Inanna, starts out the same way as Ninlil. She comes from a middle-class family. We know this because she doesn't work as a child; she's playing on the steps in front of her house when she is seen by the god Dumuzi, who falls madly in love with her and tries to seduce her. He asks her to come away with him: "We will tarry in the moonlight, we will dally in the moonshine." And she says, "But what will I tell my mother?" He responds, "I will teach you the lies that women say." (Laughter.)

But she doesn't buy any of this, and after a long courtship he has to come and ask for her hand. I mention the long courtship because the courtship of Dumuzi and Inanna was celebrated culticly—and probably also in the bars. We have lots of their love songs. If you were Sumerian and wanted to write a love song, you wrote it as Dumuzi speaking to Inanna or Inanna speaking to Dumuzi. These love songs are not going to become big hits. They don't translate very well: "Your hair is lettuce, your hair is cucumbers falling." They don't have much modern appeal. (Laughter.) But they meant a great deal to them. (Laughter.)

Ultimately, Inanna and Dumuzi get married. Their marriage is the most consequential event that ever happened for humans. Every year in Sumer, the wedding was celebrated. As far as we can tell, it was always celebrated the same way in the royal period. The male figure, who was the king and who was also Dumuzi, was brought, presumably by the men of the town, in a procession with appropriate singing to the door of the palace or the temple where Inanna dwelt. There she, played by an anonymous woman, ornamented, adorned, washed and oiled like a bride, opened the door. The two of them then disappeared into the bedroom, where they spent the night. In the morning, there was a wedding feast to which all the nobles were invited, and Inanna blessed the king and the land.

The love songs and the marriage songs reveal a great deal about the nature of this marriage and what makes Inanna different from Ninlil. One text called "Preparing the Linen Garments" is a dialogue between Inanna and her brother. He says it's time to make the wedding sheets. And she says, "Who will grow the flax for me?" He says, "I'll grow it." "Who will dry the flax for me?" "I'll dry it." "Who will stretch the flax for me? Who will beat the flax for me? Who will ret the flax for me? Who will weave the linen for me? Who will cut the cloth?" At each point her brother Utu (not Uttu, but Utu) says, "I will do it for you. I will do it for you." The last line is, "Who will sleep with me there?" And he says, "Not I, that will be your bridegroom, Dumuzi." (Laughter.)

Everybody gets a laugh. I'm sure that was true in ancient times, too. But, from all that we know from anthropology and from ancient documents, there is something wrong here. Flax making is a woman's job. Anything connected to making clothing, basically, is a woman's job. Women laid out flax even when they were old. Inanna basically says, "I'm going to get married, but don't expect me to do any of that stuff."

We have another dialogue, a wedding dialogue, between Dumuzi and Inanna in which he says to her, "I am not marrying you to be my servant. Bread you will not bake for me. Clothes you will not make for me. Food you will not cook for me. But you will sit with me at the table." Inanna is relieved of all the economic duties of a woman. Of course, wealthy women had servants to do the work, but it was their responsibility; they oversaw it. Inanna doesn't have any of those concerns, however. She has only one concern. In this same text, Dumuzi brings her before *his* gods, introduces her to the tutelary deity and prays that she will be the mother of many sons.

But she isn't! The epic literature contains references to just two minor children. And if Inanna had them, she must have had full-time nannies for them because she never turns into a mother figure. She never changes shape from the nubile young model of sexual attractiveness. She is called the "mistress of sexual attractiveness." She never turns into the antique woman with pendulous breasts and large thighs. She is eternally young and nubile—the Playboy bunny—the object of love and the personification of lust.

Not having to cook or weave or even take care of children from morning to night, she is the most incongruous of all creatures—a woman who is not kept barefoot, pregnant and in the kitchen. But she is restless. She comes to Enki, the administrator who's divvying out cosmic tasks, and says, "What have you got for me to do? You gave midwifery to Ninhursag. You gave sewing and weaving to Uttu. Why don't I have a job?" And he says, "But you are joy and lust and desire, and you are every place." And she says, in effect, "But what does that do for me?" (Chuckles.)

Inanna is portrayed as always trying to get more power. She manages, through her charm (and "hollow leg"), to become a co-administrator of the orders of the universe. She is known by the epithet of "the one who walks about." Only demons and Inanna walk about. Inanna is ferocious, the personification of blood lust, whether it is sexual blood lust or aggressive, warrior blood lust. So we have this strange creature, the undomesticated woman. She is basically unconfined. She sets out to conquer the netherworld but is trapped there and is finally rescued by the wise god Enki.

She is allowed to leave only if she delivers to the netherworld a substitute because nobody can leave the netherworld once they've been there. When Inanna leaves the realm of the dead, a retinue of sheriffs (which becomes the word for demon)—two in front, two behind, and one on each side—accompanies her. She stalks the land looking for a substitute who will be doomed to the netherworld. She comes to where her husband lives and sees that he has been playing around with every girl in the palace; she gets very mad—and sends him to the netherworld. (Laughter.)

Imagine this. It's the night of Halloween, the night of the long knives or the night of Passover. Everybody trembles in their houses while Inanna stalks the land looking for somebody to doom. And this is the goddess of joy, delight and sexuality! Somehow Freud was born a little earlier than we thought.

Inanna's husband would have been doomed to the netherworld forever, except that he has a sister who laments for him. She misses him beyond death, and she sings song after song for him. She makes such a big pest of herself that no one can stand it any more. So they decree, "Okay, *you* can take his place. Half of every year he will live here and you will go down there; the other half he will be dead." Suddenly we recognize this as an agricultural cycle of a dying and resurrected god. In fact, every year the Sumerians celebrated the birth of Dumuzi and the death of Dumuzi in the month of Tammuz (named for him). And every year they celebrated his meeting Inanna and the love songs and the sacred marriage.

Despite her powers, Inanna has no real place in the hierarchy. She's restless because women are supposed to be confined to their homes and their home duties, and she is not even occupied there. She is like a free radical—she is approachable, she floats around, and she's ready to bond. And she bonds with the highest of all humans, the King of Sumer.

From earliest recorded history, the kings of Sumer called themselves the spouse of Inanna and celebrated a sacred marriage to her. By so doing, they accomplished several things. They go back to the ritual, in which we don't know who the female is. She could be Mrs. King, but it's not said. She could be a prostitute or a priestess. Whoever she is, she is just Inanna, while the king is specifically said to be the king, and also Dumuzi.

Through the ritual, the male and female principles of the world are brought together. Culture, in the sense of urban life, represented by Inanna, and the forces within nature, represented by Dumuzi, are brought together. And the human world is related to the divine. The king is semidivine by virtue of his being the spouse of Inanna and also born of a goddess. From Inanna, who is on the periphery of the divine hierarchy, come divine blessings, including the cultural arts and agricultural fertility.

Every year this marriage is celebrated. At the wedding breakfast, the goddess Inanna announces a year of peace and abundance upon the land and security for the king. Inanna, with all her strangeness, is vital to the Sumerian understanding of the world. She is the goddess of agricultural fertility.

One of the major functions of goddesses is to be fertile. But there is no Great Goddess despite some recent claims to the contrary. Inanna is agricultural fertility; Ninhursag is the great mother and midwife, the mistress of animal and human fertility. We are so accustomed to the Bible putting together the fruits of the belly and the fruits of the land that we think of fertility as one. But the Sumerians didn't. They kept them separate. Basically, through the vagina the female force of the universe was considered determinative for the continuation of the universe—through birth by the mother goddess and through sexual encounter by the sex goddess, the madonna and the whore, if you wish.

This all changed when Sumerian civilization was overwhelmed by the Semites. Babylonian civilization brought a new synthesis. Despite what you might hear about the sexiness

of paganism, the Babylonians were prudes. They stopped celebrating the sacred marriage. Henceforth, they celebrate the
marriage of a god and his or her spouse by taking two statues
into a garden, singing a couple of songs and leaving the statues
in the garden overnight.

They also perceive the rejuvenation of the world in non-
sexual terms. Instead of celebrating the sacred marriage each
year, they develop a completely different type of mythology.
Written in Akkadian, this mythology began to have an impact
during the second half of the second millennium. In the new
Babylonian story, the Enuma Elish, formless waters co-mingle
in the beginning and ultimately evolve into gods. There are two
kinds of Babylonian gods—active gods who move around in
the air and sky, creating winds, and static gods, denizens of the
watery depths. When the winds move, they disturb the depths.
So the male water figure attacks them to try to keep them quiet,
but he is defeated by Enki. Then the mother water of us all pays
heed to her children, the gods of stasis, who complain that they
can not sleep. So she threatens the newly emergent creativity.

Suddenly the gods who were able to defeat Apsu cannot
defeat the mother water Tiamat. They are afraid even to
approach her—except for Mr. Macho—Marduk—a young god
who does not yet have a place on the divine council. Marduk is
very strong and has twice as much godliness as anybody else.
His father Enki tells him, "Come to the council. Do not bow
down. Do not show respect. March in like a warrior, and they
will listen to you." Marduk does this, and says, "I can fight for
you, you divinities of the air and sky, you with your creative
energy. After all, it's only a woman who's attacking you." A new
spirit is in the air. "If you make me king of the gods," he says,
"I will defeat her."

At this point, young Mr. Macho doesn't even have status as
a fate-determining god. He can't do anything. But the others
agree to his terms. To show him that he has moved into the
realm of the mighty and powerful, they give him the power of

the creative word. They say, "Speak." He speaks and a constellation comes into being. They say, "Speak again." He speaks and the constellation disappears.

So, armed with weapons of the storm and the wind, Marduk goes to fight the mother goddess Tiamat. They meet in single combat—and he defeats her. When she opens her mouth to swallow him, he blows her up with his winds. She becomes big as a balloon. He then takes his arrow of lightning and pierces her. A very ignoble ending. Then he takes her body and creates the universe, providing a permanent place for the gods so that each one knows his place, and there will be order in the universe, a differentiated world.

He then establishes a hierarchical state, where everybody knows *his* function, everybody has *his* place. I say "his" because there are no goddesses in this tale, just gods. They are the state and the governors. In order to support this system, so the male gods won't have to work, he conceives of the brilliant idea of creating an underclass, which is us, to do all the work. And every year his victory over disorder is celebrated as the governing principle of the world. As long as hierarchy, domination and order subdue the rash natural elements of the cosmos, the world is safe for another year.

This is not monotheism. This is classically developed polytheism. The same story, with some variations, is found in Canaan, among the Hittites and among the Greeks. The mythology of the last half of the second millennium tells of a world of power, hierarchy, status and the orderly control of things. And women have no place in this hierarchy.

Goddesses have no place in it. Goddesses are either trivialized into "consorts," Mrs. Gods, "first ladies," or domesticated, called upon in private situations, like the mother goddess at childbirth. The only goddess who escapes this eclipse is Inanna, who is called Ishtar by the Babylonians. Unable to be domesticated by her very nature, she becomes a major warrior goddess. At the same time, she makes men look beyond their roles in the cosmos to the messy stuff of home and procreation, something they wouldn't do if they really were orderly creatures.

What we find in developed paganism, in other words, in the religion of all the cultures that surrounded Israel, is *not* feminist religion but models of patriarchy and the patriarchal state. The divine image of patriarchy is of a king of the gods who sits on his throne, uses his power and collects his tribute.

Does this have anything to do with Israel? Yes and no. Israel has a fundamentally different system, in which the gender line is totally ignored or obscured. Rather than presenting a model of how women should be controlled, Israelite theology doesn't talk about women at all. We can argue *ad infinitum* about which is worse for women—to be dominated explicitly or to be ignored and rendered invisible. But without female principles, the nature of God undergoes a major transformation. God ceases to be phallic. You do not see God below the waist. There is no mention of God's fertility as coming from his loins. On the contrary, everything is cerebralized into the divine word, and God becomes a talking torso.

This change has major implications. On the one hand, it removes the warrant for male domination. But, as you know, history and culture rushed in to project male domination onto the religious base anyway and to imagine God with a phallus. But the ordering of the world, the essential running of the world, is desexualized, as it already was in Babylonian mythology of the late second millennium. God now has all the powers, even the domestic power of the birth goddess. As those of you who read Scripture know, the Bible tells us over and over that God controls birth—he stops up wombs, he opens wombs, he forms the baby in the womb, he determines the destiny of the baby, he sees the baby in the womb. God does everything.

But if God does everything and God has all the power, why does anything ever happen? In paganism, the world is always in flux—god against god, god cooperating with god, gods merging with each other, fighting with each other. You can see why things happen. In monotheism, why should God ever do anything? It could be a static world. What happens in the Bible is that the role of humanity expands beyond anything imagined in paganism.

In the Bible, the creature is created as a creature. So far, we could be in Mesopotamia. But the creature is restless and determined to grow. The creature grabs for wisdom. The goddess Uttu taught humans how to make clothes; Eve discovers it on her own. The first couple eat the apple, their eyes are opened, and they sew themselves garments. Through eating they learn how to sew, they change from natural beings into cultural beings. The next step is agriculture. They leave the garden and become farmers.

In the genealogies of the first 11 chapters of Genesis, all the arts of civilization are developed by humankind. They are all born with us, including kingship. In Mesopotamia, kingship is a gift of the gods, as are smithing and artwork and song. Not in Genesis. There a formidable creature is developing. By the end of Genesis 11, the creature is so powerful that nothing can hinder it. It goes forth, is scattered over the whole world and builds a universe.

This creature is God's counterpart, God's *tselem*, the very image of God. In Mesopotamia, this term applies only to the king, who is God's foil. In the Bible, it applies to all humans. Humanity, in the persona of Israel, determines the fate of the world by how human beings order their *own* culture. If human beings are good to each other, there will be abundant rain. If they do not lead ethical lives, the prophets tell us, the earth will dry up and mourn, and the heavens will cease to rain. First, Israel will be lost, and, second, humanity will disappear from the cosmos. The issue—the difference between paganism and Israelite monotheism—is stark. We are no longer sitting in the bleachers rooting for our favorite gods in the divine soccer game. We are the players.

Is there room for goddesses here? Is there room for women? It depends on who you ask, and when. For as long as they could, human beings tried to escape the radical monotheism of Deuteronomy, in which human beings determine whether or not there will be births. Only in the last 10 or 15 years, with holes in the ozone and increasing pollution and nuclear threats and biological mutations and new viruses, has it become hard to escape the idea that humans determine the fate of the universe. And we had better do so consciously, because we do so unconsciously anyway.

But before we became so powerful that the results of our actions stared us in the face, we ran from our responsibility, partly by developing a theology of repentance. We could come to God and say, "Gee, I'm sorry, I broke it." And God would fix it. Repentance became very important in the development of the image of God the Father, God who chastises but also accepts repentance. We developed the parable of the Prodigal Son who returns and other patterns of redemption through sacrifice, atonement and repentance. We find this idea both in temple theology and later in early Christianity and Judaism.

The search for ways to influence the Father to forgive us and, therefore, correct our mistakes also encompassed a search for anyone who could influence the Father on our behalf—for example, the prophet, whose job was to pray for Israel; the priest, whose job was to offer sacrifices. But why stop there? The dead, too, could intercede, especially mother Rachel. In Jeremiah's famous vision, mother Rachel, the mother of the northern tribes, has been mourning, loudly, without stopping, for 150 years. She cannot be comforted. Finally God says, "Okay, I'm going to reward your labor, your children will come back." So we look for a mother in Zion, the city herself, who opens her arms in the books of Lamentation and begins an incessant noise-making and crying to soften God's heart, to bring the people back.

Our search for anyone who can intervene with God becomes the search for a beloved intermediary, Lady Wisdom, who unites us with God in our joint love for her, or Lady

Jerusalem, who marries both God and Israel in the perfect eschaton and thereby conjoins them. Are these echoes of goddesses, who survived in some subterranean fashion? Or are these new manifestations of the same psychological and sociological phenomenon that gave rise to the goddesses in the first place?

Goddesses are mediators. Women are always mediators. Miriam is a mediator. You pray to your mother to help you with your father. You may pray to your father to help you with your mother, but if the father has the power, then you pray to your mother to help you. The development of female intercessors reaches a peak in the glorification of Mary; the Jewish counterpart is the devotion and pilgrimages to the tomb of Rachel.

It's hard to say if Lady Wisdom is a survival of the great goddesses of wisdom of the third and early second millennium or if she and the goddesses of wisdom are the result of our experiences in the first few years of life, when the wise one, who brings us into civilization and teaches us to eat food and wear clothes and go to the potty, is our mother, who, at some point, is all-wise in our eyes. Or is Lady Wisdom a cultural memory that in earlier times, when forests had to be cleared and trenches had to be dug and oxen had to be guided and horses had to be tamed, the upper-body strength of men dictated that they would do the physical activity, which meant that everything else—cooking, sewing, pottery making, beer making— would be done by women? Of course, this "everything else" seems a little bit magical and more sophisticated, and women developed the reputation of having access to secret knowledge. We don't know whether these are echoes or resonances.

In the time that remains, I want to focus on another aspect of this potential echoing. Goddesses are patrons of certain arts. In every pagan religion, humanity learns civilization from the gods. Everything is a gift from the gods, who oversee what you do and give you the skill to do it. If you look at what is associated with female gods and what is associated with male gods, you find an interesting pattern. The immediate transformational activities—making clothes, food, beer—are associated with goddesses because those are the things mothers do.

But goddesses are also mistresses of the obscure, the mantic arts, divination, riddle solving. Perhaps, this reflects the role of the mother in early childhood and the role of women in early economic systems. You want a dream interpreted? Speak to your goddess. Even Gilgamesh, when he needs a dream interpreted, asks his mother, Ninsun. You want to send a sage to a foreign army? If you live in the third millennium, the sage may very well be a woman.

So the cultural arts, the mantic arts, singing and dancing are all associated with females (although, to some extent, also with males). In Sumerian paganism, one particular god grows and grows and finally absorbs all of the cultural arts and the wisdom of the female deities. He is the god Enki.

But when we look at the Bible, we find something very interesting. In a patriarchal world where men were the major actors, in a world where women were not so much shackled as they were limited by the felt need to control their sexuality, despite all of the androcentric focus in the Bible, women keep cropping up as figures from the margin who know what should happen and who do whatever is necessary to make sure it happens.

Eve is just the first of many women who transform the human situation. She reaches for the fruit because she is fascinated by its ability to make one wise. But she isn't very different from mother Rebecca, who is privy to an oracle (which, apparently, wasn't given to Isaac) that Jacob, rather than Esau, is to be the inheritor, and who uses every means in her power to affect that outcome. Sarah also uses her power to insure that Isaac will be the heir. In her case we're not told if she knows this is in accord with the divine will, but with Rebecca we are told quite clearly that she knows. During the period of the Exodus, we find women acting independently. Miriam supervises and knows what's going to happen. Zipporah, Moses' wife, knows what to do when God attacks.

When we look at the historical books of the Bible, this pattern becomes regularized and clear. The first story in the historical books, in Joshua 2, is the story of Rahab, the prostitute of Jericho. Rahab, the marginal of the marginal, a prostitute of a foreign people, proclaims the divine decree; she is the one who tells Israel God will give them the land. At the end of the historical books, another woman, Hulda the prophetess, proclaims that Israel's occupation of the land will soon come to an end, at least temporarily. She is also the one who proclaims the validity or authoritativeness of the book of the Law we call Deuteronomy. In between, a female medium makes the pronouncement that Saul's reign is about to end and David's about to begin.

Whether these are echoes of the mantic rites of the goddesses or reflections of the psychological attachment to mother, we cannot say. But we should note that the Bible is consistently bracketed and punctuated by the wise words of women.

O ur next speaker is going to ask some difficult questions— the really tough ones. What if we can't reclaim a biblical text? And what's the history of the struggle to open the Bible to women?

Pamela Milne is associate professor of religious studies at the University of Windsor in Ontario, Canada. She received her Ph.D. at Magill University and has done extensive research in Jerusalem at both the Ecole Biblique et Archeologique Francaise and the William F. Albright School of Archaeological Research. She has also done research at Hebrew Union College and the University of Michigan.

Professor Milne has published widely on feminist issues, and I must say, she manages to find the deeper issues in whatever she touches. For example, her next published paper is going to explore "gynophobic images"—that means women-hating images—in certain biblical texts. She questions our assumptions, and she makes us think. It's a pleasure for me to introduce to you Pamela Milne, who will speak to us on rejecting the authority of the Bible. —H.S.

No Promised Land: Rejecting the Authority of the Bible

PAMELA J. MILNE

In Western culture, the Bible has provided the single most important sustaining rationale for the oppression of women. The very structures of our societies are heavily indebted to the Bible in areas such as law, family, sexual mores and, of course, religion. Because these structures have institutionalized the second-class status of women, the focus of the feminist movement has been on fostering the kinds of changes that will improve the status of women.

From the very beginning of the feminist movement to the present, the authority of Scripture has frequently been invoked by opponents in an effort to slow down or stop this kind of social change. This use of the Bible is rooted in the belief that as the word of God the Bible prescribes certain things, including a hierarchical relationship between men and women. Variations from prescribed forms and relationships are regarded as deviations from the divine will and, therefore, wrong.

Unlike most other literary collections, the Bible has an uninterrupted and extensive history of interpretation stretching over millennia. With few exceptions, this interpretive tradition understands the Bible in a thoroughly patriarchal way.

Patriarchy and Sexism

Before going any further, I should take a moment to define the terms "patriarchy" and "sexism" because they will occur throughout my discussion of feminist approaches to the Bible. Feminists generally use the term "patriarchy" to refer to the manifestation and institutionalization of male dominance over women and children. The term is derived from Greco-Roman law, wherein the male head of the household had absolute power over all other members of the household. Of course, this system of male dominance *existed* long before the Greeks and Romans.[1] They just gave it clear legal articulation.

The concept of patriarchy is closely linked to another concept, sexism. The term "sexism" refers to the ideology of male supremacy. Sexism is the set of beliefs that establishes and sustains patriarchal institutions and systems.[2] One typical manifestation of sexism and patriarchy is the separation of the public and domestic spheres. In a patriarchal society, men confine women to the domestic sphere, over which they exercise control, while they reserve the public domain almost exclusively for themselves. Believing themselves to be intellectually, morally and physically superior to women, men deem themselves better suited to hold all or most of the civil and religious leadership and decision-making roles that govern society. In this way, they exercise control over women as a group.

The desire to control women's sexuality and fertility seems to be one of the central underlying goals of patriarchal society and is accomplished by limiting women's freedom of access to the public sphere, as well as women's legal rights as persons. (Women didn't become persons in Canadian law until 1929.)

The Bible and Patriarchy

All the societies in the ancient Mediterranean world during the period in which the biblical tradition was formed were patriarchal. It is not remarkable or unexpected, therefore, that a document produced in that context expresses the view that men are superior to women and that women are the property of men. Indeed, it would be remarkable if this were *not* the case. If the Bible is remarkable, it is because the expression of patriarchy is *more*, rather than less, pronounced than what is found in religious texts produced by surrounding cultures. Were it not for the fact that the Bible, as a fixed collection of texts, has been regarded by so many people as divinely inspired, and thus authoritative, the contents would be a matter of historical and literary interest only.

Those who were responsible for declaring the Bible the authoritative word of God surely never imagined a world beyond patriarchy, a world in which women would claim equality as they are now doing. But such a world is in the process of emerging. The Bible, which seems to offer a critique of some other forms of oppression, seems to *promote* sexual oppression. There is certainly no lack of evidence to show that many people who oppose women in their struggle for equality appeal to the Bible for divine support of their views.

David Clines has observed that "the biblical text is in conflict with a principle that is not a passing fancy of the modern world but has become a fundamental way of looking at the world," namely, that "women are fully human...and that the issue of [sexual equality] is...something we have to get right if we want to be serious people."[3] So serious people, especially feminist people, are having to reassess their relationship to the authoritative status of the Bible as a guide for structuring relationships between men and women in the modern world. To the extent that the very concept of authority is itself a construct of the patriarchal order, feminists need to ask if the Bible serves any useful feminist purpose. My answer to this question is a resounding no.

Although patriarchy was certainly not invented by the authors of the Bible, most feminists, including most feminist biblical scholars, now concede that patriarchy is deeply ingrained in the Bible. In the early stages of feminism, many feminist theologians and biblical scholars hoped that an essential Bible could be separated from its patriarchal dimensions, that a nonpatriarchal canon-within-the-canon could be extracted from the whole and reclaimed for use in the future egalitarian feminist world. Today, that hope has all but disappeared, and other strategies for salvaging a nonpatriarchal, authoritative tradition are being explored. In my view, these new strategies not only are proving unsuccessful, but they have intensified the dilemma for those who want to identify themselves as Jewish feminists and Christian feminists, rather than simply as feminists.

Although I think feminists should abandon the idea of an authoritative Scripture because it is more detrimental than beneficial to women seeking equality, I emphatically do not think feminists should abandon study of the Bible. Feminist analysis of the Bible and the history of biblical interpretation can make an important contribution to the contemporary feminist movement. In fact, I would argue that no other literary text in the Western world is more in need of feminist criticism than the Bible.

Not many seem to appreciate the importance of this task, however, because feminist biblical scholars find themselves somewhat between a rock and a hard place. The rock is the negative reaction to critical investigation of the Bible, especially feminist criticism, from the religious right. And the hard place is the chilly indifference of many feminists toward feminist biblical scholarship.

Raising critical questions about the Bible has always been a dangerous activity. We need only think about the trouble Galileo got himself into by using the newly developed telescope to prove the theory that the earth revolved around the sun. Science notwithstanding, there were powerful men who believed that the Bible taught otherwise, and Galileo's work was condemned. He spent the last decade of his life under house arrest. It took more than 300 years to clear his name in the Catholic church.

Even issues that had far less cosmic significance could endanger a scholar's life or career. For example, prior to the Protestant Reformation, suggesting that Moses may not have been the sole author of the Torah (the first five books of the Bible) was something scholars only dared to do in vague, veiled or posthumous ways out of fear for their reputations, their jobs or their freedom.

If critical scholarship involving the Bible has sometimes been a dangerous enterprise for male scholars in the past, it should not be surprising to learn that critical feminist scholarship harbors difficulties and dangers for women scholars today. Feminism, after all, may be the most important revolutionary development since the Copernican revolution.[4] Like the Copernican revolution, it is changing the very way we understand our world. It is changing what we regard as central and peripheral. Whereas the claim that the earth revolved around the sun threatened the centrality of man's place in the universe, the feminist assertion of women's equality threatens the centrality of man's place even on earth. It is not a threat that is taken lightly.

Until very recently, just being a feminist scholar diminished employment prospects at all but the most progressive academic institutions. But the dangers of being a feminist *biblical* scholar can go well beyond this. The stakes can be quite high, high enough to bring threats of violence. The next speaker, Jane Schaberg, is a case in point. Her thought-provoking work on stories about the birth of Jesus, along with her work on Mary Magdalene, have produced hate mail (male?), death threats and worse.

Last year, after an article on her research appeared in the *Detroit Free Press*, someone set fire to her car while it was parked in the driveway of her residence. I think her work has drawn such extreme hostile reactions because it touches directly, and in such a challenging way, on the central patriarchal paradigms of womanhood in Christianity. Many people, even in a society as secular as this one, take the Bible, or at least their understanding of it, very seriously. The application of feminist principles to study of the Bible can, therefore, be perceived as extremely threatening.

But, in addition to hostility from those who oppose feminism or critical biblical scholarship, or a combination of the two, feminists who work with the Bible experience an additional and unusual problem. Feminist biblical scholarship is looked upon with suspicion, even disdain, perhaps as much by other feminists as by traditionalists, though for very different reasons.

Gerda Lerner, in her book *The Creation of Patriarchy*, illustrates this attitude quite clearly. She criticizes feminist biblical scholars such as Phyllis Trible, Phyllis Bird and John Otwell for trying "to balance the overwhelming evidence of patriarchal domination [in the Bible] by citing examples of a few female heroic figures or women who take independent action of one sort or another." Such examples, in Lerner's opinion, are insufficient to prove that women had either a high status or a status equal to men in the biblical tradition.[5]

The uneasiness of other feminist scholars toward feminist work on the Bible arises from the suspicion that no matter how sexist the Bible proves to be, the majority of feminist biblical scholars will defend the religious authority and spiritual value of the Bible. As Letty Russell, a Christian feminist theologian, puts it, feminist biblical scholars remain "marginal to a great deal of feminist scholarship because they continue to uphold the value of biblical materials in spite of their patriarchal bias against women."[6]

Other feminists suspect that feminist biblical scholars subordinate the ideology of feminism to the sexist ideology of the Bible and biblical tradition when they acknowledge the Bible as religiously authoritative. So the issue of the authority of the Bible, I believe, needs to be addressed more directly. In order to see where we stand with this issue now, I want to examine what I regard as some of the key strategic developments in feminist approaches to the Bible.

Two Hundred Years of Feminist Interpretation

Many people are not aware that in this country feminist efforts to counteract the use of the Bible in the oppression of women are as old as the feminist movement itself, which goes back at least 200 years to the end of the 18th century. Within these 200 years, there have been two distinct waves of feminism separated by a gap of about 40 years, from about 1920 to the 1960s, when feminist activism was diminished.

Between the first and second waves of feminism, a change seems to have occurred in the role played by feminist analysis of the Bible in the feminist movement as a whole. In the first phase of feminism, a feminist critique of the Bible and Bible-based religions, especially Christianity, was deemed essential by some of the most prominent leaders of the feminist movement. In the current phase, the work of feminist biblical criticism has become rather peripheral. One reason for this change is, no doubt, that Christianity provided the operating framework for 19th-century America to a greater extent than it does today.

Stepping outside a traditional religious framework would have been more difficult then than it is now; at least it would have been less socially acceptable. Today, many feminists regard the Bible, and the religious systems connected with it, as largely irrelevant, neither a help nor too much of a hindrance to the central tasks of transforming legal, political and educational systems.

The First Phase
The first phase of the women's rights movement directed its energies at liberating women from the constraints of the domestic sphere. In particular, this meant women having access to education equal to the education available to men, gaining the right to participate in the public debate on major social issues and securing the right to vote.

The work of Judith Sargent Murray, a liberal Universalist from Massachusetts, is often cited as marking the beginning of the women's rights movement in the United States.[7] Murray was among the first to advocate equal educational opportunities for women. She was also one of the first to challenge traditional interpretations of the Bible, which were offered in defense of the *status quo*. When she published her essay "On the Equality of the Sexes" in 1790, Murray appended a passage written ten years earlier to a male friend.

From that extract, we learn that her views on education for women had already met with opposition. Furthermore, we learn that the Bible was being used as a proof-text for women's inferiority and subordination to men. The ultimate argument for denying women the same education as men was, apparently, that God had created women as secondary and inferior beings. Therefore, they did *not merit* the same education as men.

Murray's male friend must have used the Adam-Eve story in Genesis 2–3 as his primary supporting evidence for the theory of male superiority because, in her response to him, Murray provides her own, somewhat mocking, and very nontraditional interpretation of that story.[8] She summed up her interpretation of the text with this taunt:

> Thus it would seem, that all the arts of the grand deceiver…were requisite to mislead our general mother, while the father of mankind forfeited his own, and relinquished the happiness of posterity, merely in compliance with the blandishments of a female.[9]

It is not difficult to guess how Murray's friend had used the Adam-Eve story because it had such a clearly established place in Christian theologies of woman. Although the Hebrew biblical tradition virtually ignored it,[10] the story took on new life in the intertestamental period, when it was taken up in early Jewish writings but became especially important in Christian writings.

As the story was elaborated, the character of Adam was idealized while Eve became the source of evil and the cause of man's fall.[11] Christian theologians through the centuries, both Catholic and Protestant, constructed theologies of women primarily on the basis of this text. These theologies typically depict woman as secondary and inferior to man because she was created after him.

The interpretation of this text and its negative application to women are well represented in the writings of the second-century Christian author, Tertullian (c. 160–240 C.E.). To Tertullian, every woman is Eve, and Eve is the devil's gateway and the destroyer of man, who is the image of God. It is because of Eve that Christ had to die.[12] It is hard to imagine a heavier guilt trip than the one laid on Christian women with this use of the text.

More than a thousand years later, the same story provided the justification for executing many women as witches. Women were thought to be prone to witchcraft because witchcraft comes from carnal lust, and carnal lust has been insatiable in women from the time of Eve onward. For it was Eve, not the devil, who seduced Adam, and for this reason she is more bitter than death.[13] By Judith Sargent Murray's time, there was probably no other biblical text that had a more concrete, negative impact on women's lives. Murray's attempt at reinterpreting the Adam-Eve story did not meet with approval from male clergymen, many of whom found the very idea of a woman interpreting Scripture highly offensive.

By the middle of the 19th century, another area of conflict had emerged. Women who attempted to participate in the public debate around the practice of slavery again found the Bible being used to exclude them. Quaker women in particular had become quite prominent in the abolitionist movement. These women organized women's antislavery associations, wrote booklets for women urging them to support the abolitionist movement and lectured on the subject to groups of women in private homes. The work of Angelina Grimké was especially popular. Her lectures in New England drew large audiences of women.

But when men began attending her lectures, she roused the wrath of the orthodox clergy. Women were not to speak or teach in public. To these religious gentlemen, it was clear from 1 Timothy 2:9–14 that women should not teach or have authority over men. They should, instead, be silent and submissive. As wives, they should be submissive to their husbands

(1 Peter 3:1–7; Ephesians 5:21–24; Colossians 3: 18–19). The Council of Congregationalist Ministers of Massachusetts issued a pastoral letter in 1837, which reads in part:

> The appropriate duties and influence of women are clearly stated in the New Testament. Those duties and that influence are unobtrusive and private but the source of mighty power....The power of woman is her dependence, flowing from the weakness which God has given her for her protection....We cannot, therefore, but regret the mistaken conduct of those who encourage females to bear an obtrusive and ostentatious part in measures of reform, and countenance any of that sex who forget themselves as to itinerate in the character of public lecturers and teachers.[14]

(They wouldn't have attended this seminar!) Others found more physical ways of expressing their displeasure. Wherever Angelina or her sister Sarah spoke, they could expect to encounter opponents hurling stones and rotten eggs at them, along with verbal abuse.[15]

The use of the Bible as a weapon against women's public activities forced women in the antislavery movement to take up the issue of women's rights in the context of biblical interpretation. Sarah Grimké herself entered the debate, charging that the arguments put forward by the clergy were based upon false translations, perverted interpretations and usurped authority.[16]

At the Seneca Falls Convention of 1848, the first women's rights convention, the role of the Bible and institutionalized religion in the oppression of women was a topic of discussion, and women began the task of analyzing the Bible from a feminist perspective in more earnest. The struggle between the women's movement and the churches now centered on political enfranchisement, the right to vote. Once again, all the biblical prooftexts were trotted out in an effort to show that the ballot box was *not* the proper sphere of women. Catholic spokesman Orestes

Brownson proclaimed that women's suffrage would destroy the Christian family. (Interestingly, the liquor industry, worried about the effect of the women's temperance movement, was as keen to prevent women from voting as were the churches.)[17]

Most feminists, on the other hand, were convinced that the Bible was being misused. They felt certain that when correctly interpreted the Bible would provide no evidence of female inferiority or subordination to men. Some feminists, like Lucy Stone, studied Greek and Hebrew so they could read the Scriptures in the original languages for themselves. But their efforts were not very successful in reducing opposition to the idea of women's equality in the major Christian churches. On the contrary, opponents of women's suffrage succeeded in excluding women from the Fifteenth Amendment, which extended voting rights to black men (1869).

Toward the end of the 19th century, still striving to obtain the right to vote and still experiencing opposition from organized religion, feminists seem to have taken two different paths. One path was to ignore religious opposition altogether; the other was to confront it more directly. Two of the central leaders of the women's suffrage movement, Matilda Joslyn Gage and Elizabeth Cady Stanton, chose the latter path because they were convinced from their many years in the women's movement that the Bible had been a powerful and effective weapon in the war against women's rights.

Up to this point, feminists had taken the view that the problem was not with the Bible itself but with male misinterpretation of the Bible. Feminist critics had relied on two main strategies. The first was to counter traditional interpretations of texts like Genesis 2–3 with women-positive interpretations. The second was to counter negative female characters, such as Jezebel, with positive ones, such as Miriam and Deborah.

Gage and Stanton, however, reached a different conclusion. They were convinced that the Bible *itself* was the problem. The Bible could be used effectively against women because it was a patriarchal document containing degrading teachings about women. The new task for feminist biblical criticism, therefore, was to expose the Bible for what it was and to counteract the influence of organized religion on women's lives.

In her book *Women, Church and State: The Exposé of Male Collaboration Against the Female Sex* (1893), Matilda Gage charged that belief in the secondary and subordinate status of women is a cornerstone of Christianity, a component inherited from Judaism. The oppression of women, in her view, was part of the fabric of the religion and not simply a cultural element that could be overcome through reinterpretation. Gage also observed that women's increasing freedoms throughout the preceding hundred years had been won in spite of, rather than because of, the Christian church.[18]

Two years later, in 1895, Elizabeth Cady Stanton published *The Woman's Bible*, in which she examined all biblical texts pertaining to women (or at least the ones she thought pertained to women). By the end of this exercise, Stanton had come to the conclusion that the Bible contains degrading teachings about women and that these teachings form the foundation of the Christian view of women.[19] Having reached this conclusion, Stanton tried to convince women not to regard the Bible as the word of God but to regard it merely as a collection of historical and mythological writings by men. If the Bible is not divinely ordained, women are under no moral obligation to accept its directives.[20]

Not surprisingly, the religious establishment did not welcome her views. In fact, the clergy denounced Stanton's book as scandalous, a work of the devil.[21] What was surprising, however, was that *The Woman's Bible* received a very cool reception from many feminists. The leadership of the suffrage movement had been taken over by young, wealthy and conservative women who were concerned that such a work would damage the credibility of the movement. In 1896, the National American Suffrage Association voted to disavow any connection with Stanton's work.[22] This seems to mark the end of the first period of feminist biblical interpretation. The conclusions reached by Gage and Stanton seemed too frightening to pursue.

Second Phase

During the first period, feminists studied the Bible out of necessity, and their critique was an essential part of the struggle for women's rights, but few of them had professional training in biblical scholarship. By the time feminists took up the study of the Bible again, in the 1970s, there had been some important changes.

Women now had much greater access to theological training. As a result, those who studied the Bible did so as professional biblical scholars and theologians. Critical study of the Bible, however, no longer seemed to have a central place in the feminist movement. The work of feminist biblical scholars seemed less directly connected to the social revolution and more connected to the theological and academic worlds.

What had not changed appreciably, either in society as a whole or within the mainline churches, was the understanding of the Bible's teaching on women. After a century of feminist effort, traditional antiwoman interpretations remained the norm.

The work of Phyllis Trible on the Adam-Eve story is usually cited as marking the beginning of the second phase of feminist biblical criticism. And I really can't emphasize too strongly the influence Professor Trible has had in shaping the second phase. In tackling Genesis 2–3, Trible picked up where 19th-century feminists, prior to Gage and Stanton, had left off. She focused on the Bible as a literary text and examined its content, language and rhetorical structures.

Like many of her 19th-century sisters, Trible undertakes her work from inside a Christian faith context. She tries to demonstrate, in more convincing ways than before, that the Adam-Eve story has been seriously misinterpreted through the centuries. Words have been misunderstood, organizing structures have gone unnoticed, and the silences of the text have been filled with male-biased speculations.

At times, Trible sounds very much like Murray in mocking the tendency of male interpreters to fill in the blanks with male-serving musings. How might the story have been understood if women had been doing the speculating over the centuries, she asks. The text doesn't say why the serpent approached the woman instead of the man, but women could tell you it was because the woman was more intelligent—she was the theologian and translator. Why did the man eat the fruit offered to him by the woman? Because he was belly-oriented.[23] You get the point.

Like most of her feminist predecessors, Trible locates the antiwoman problem more in the interpreter than in the text itself. Although she readily concedes that the patriarchal stamp of Scripture is permanent, she remains convinced that the intentionality of biblical faith is not patriarchal. For her, the intentionality of biblical faith is salvation—for men and women.

In addition to identifying this intentionality in Genesis 2-3, Trible has worked on numerous other biblical texts, such as Ruth and the Song of Songs, which have not been as habitually used against women by male theologians over the centuries. These texts do not need to be "rescued" in the same sense as Genesis 2-3. They provide a counterbalance—Song of Songs by redeeming the love story gone awry in the garden and Ruth by telling a woman's story in a man's world and thereby transforming the male culture it reflects. As Trible reads these and several other biblical texts through her feminist lens, she finds them placing patriarchal culture under judgment and affirming the equality of male and female.

But there are other stories, she readily concedes, that can not be rescued or understood this way. These are the "texts of terror" that describe women being abused, raped, mutilated and murdered—women like Hagar, Jephthah's daughter and the Levite's concubine. These stories she neither excuses nor attempts to reclaim but focuses, instead, on the suffering of the female victims. She calls for repentance in the hope that such horrors will not be repeated.

In all of her work, Trible, to her credit, has been both open and clear about her interpretive goals. As a consciously ideological approach, feminist work should be done for the benefit of women in some way, but not all of us are as frank as Trible about the purposes of our work. She is a Christian feminist who loves the Bible, despite the fact, to use her words, that "evidence abounds for the subordination, inferiority and abuse of women."[24] Believing there are dimensions of the Bible that can be separated from patriarchy, the niche she claims for her work is that of redeeming the past (an ancient document) and the present (its continuing use) from the confines of patriarchy.[25] Although the canon as traditionally formulated is not acceptable to her, she does think feminist canons-within-the-canon can be established.[26]

Much feminist work on the Bible has followed Trible's lead. In the interests of time, I will mention just a few illustrative examples drawn from the Hebrew Scriptures. These examples in no way represent the many directions and interpretive strategies being used today by feminist biblical scholars. They only highlight what I perceive to be the ongoing problem presented to feminists by the notion of the authority of the Bible. Considerable work has been done by Jewish and Christian feminist scholars on a wide range of biblical texts, including Ruth, Esther, the Song of Songs, Lady Wisdom and Judith (one of the books of the Apocrypha, which is part of the canon for Roman Catholics), in an effort to discover countercultural, woman-liberating dimensions within the Bible.[27]

Although this work goes on, there has been a shift in emphasis by many feminist scholars away from the reclamation project. Optimism about its viability has diminished, and many have turned to the task of exposing the full dimensions of patriarchal ideology in the Bible without making any attempt to rescue the Bible from this ideology.

Initially, there were just a few who voiced feminist doubts about the recoverability of women-positive dimensions. Esther Fuchs was the most notable as she explored the subtle ways patriarchy was expressed through biblical texts. Her suspicions were that patriarchal ideology went much deeper than the words on the page. In one study, she examined the motif of deception and discovered that although both male and female characters make use of deception they do so for different motives, and their actions are evaluated on different bases.

Deception is more of a defining characteristic for women in the Bible than for men, and it is a characteristic that promotes male fear of women. Good women use deception to benefit their Israelite menfolk, while bad women use deception to benefit themselves. Men, on the other hand, can deceive for their own benefit and still be evaluated positively. This gender-biased use of the deception motif was an important factor, Fuchs argued, that contributed to the growing gynophobia—fear of women—that seems so powerful and pervasive in writings from the post-Exilic period.[28]

Soon, others were also bringing a hermeneutic of suspicion to their reading of the biblical text. In Gale Yee's work on Proverbs 1–9, she raised doubts about Lady Wisdom. Rather than detaching this figure from her context, as many others had done, Yee looked at how she was contrasted with another female figure, the Strange Woman. The voices of these two women are described as being so similar that a man has difficulty telling one from the other. The choice is critical, however, because following the voice of Wisdom brings life but being seduced by the voice of the Strange Woman brings death. Although some see positive value in the image of Wisdom as a woman, Yee alerted us to the ways this text pits women against women and encourages male fear of women. The Strange Woman bears a remarkable resemblance to ordinary women whose voices become voices of seduction seeking to destroy men.[29]

Other feminists are now raising questions about whether the story of Esther is suitable for inclusion in a woman's canon-within-the-canon. Is Esther really the kind of role model feminists want to promote? Itumeleng Mosala is among those who have recently reassessed this text. As a black, feminist, South African scholar, she wanted to see what such a story might contribute to black women's struggle for liberation in the South African context. Her conclusion is that this biblical text does not support women in their struggle, not only because it uses a female character to achieve patriarchal ends, but also because it sacrifices gender issues to nationalist issues and suppresses the issue of class altogether.[30]

The suitability of the Song of Songs has also been called into question. Trible's work was groundbreaking on this text, too. And many share her view that the Song is a symphony of love in which there is no male dominance or female subordination.[31] In the introduction to a recently published volume, *A Feminist Companion to the Song of Songs*, Athalya Brenner claims that "there is virtual consent among scholars today that some...of the poetry of the Song of Songs should probably be attributed to female perspectives or even authorship." In Brenner's view, the social attitudes expressed in this text are "generally non-sexist," and the female figure and voice are prominent.[32]

But cracks have even begun to appear in the feminist consensus about this text. A recent study of the Song of Songs by David Clines illustrates this shift.[33] Not only does he challenge the suggestion of female authorship, a theory that is tenuous at best, but he also finds this a very sexist text, one that is especially dangerous because the sexism is insidious. "A more blatantly sexist text," he argues, "would do less damage than one that beguiles." According to Clines, both the author and audience are male and Israelite.

Drawing on the work of Fredric Jameson, Clines argues that this text, like all texts, owes its existence to a desire to repress social conflict, a desire to allow oppressors to deny their role as oppressors and to enable the oppressed to forget their suffering. The desire of the male author of the Song of Songs is to repress the conflict of interest between the sexes by providing a literary representation of male and female lovers who are more or less equal. This literary representation masks the reality that in ancient Israel, as in most societies known to us, men as a group have power over women as a group, and women have virtually no power outside the domestic setting within which they are regarded as men's property. As Clines reads it, the Song of Songs is actually a man's dream about a woman's love, a dream about a woman who is forward in love-making but who does nothing all day but fantasize about him. The woman in this text is not a real woman. She is a male-constructed woman, constructed precisely to serve the needs of the patriarchal system.

The character of Judith has also attracted attention, particularly from Roman Catholic scholars, as another text that might offer a women-positive role model. Judith, you will recall, saves the Jewish people from destruction by the Assyrians by seducing the Assyrian general, Holofernes, into a drunken stupor, cutting off his head with his own sword and carrying it back to the townsmen of Bethulia to be displayed on the town wall. Several biblical scholars, some of them feminist, have described Judith as a feminist heroine or a feminist kind of heroine. Elisabeth Schüssler Fiorenza, for example, reads the story as a heroic biography based on feminist irony.

In my own work on Judith, I attempt to show that feminists should be wary of promoting a story or character like Judith. Although Judith acts with uncharacteristic independence and heroism, she is a character who is completely male-imaged, a woman who presents herself from a thoroughly male perspective and serves only the needs and interests of the men of the community and their male-imaged god. Moreover, Judith's actions revolve around the dynamics of men's fear of women's seductive powers.

The "warrior" role that Judith plays is the role of the *femme fatale*. Her voice and body are the weapons she uses to destroy a man, just as the father in Proverbs 1–9 had warned his son the Strange Woman would do. Judith is praised because she unleashes these weapons only against an enemy. She does not harm her own because she is a man's woman who can do only what her male creator allows. But a male reader of the story understands that without such literary constraints real women may not be as selective about which men they destroy. As a character, Judith promotes fear of women and women's sexuality, not the equality of women, to male readers for whom the story was written.[34]

While feminists have been giving sober second thoughts to texts that looked like promising candidates for a woman-friendly canon, they are also having doubts about Trible's reinterpretations of Genesis 2–3. Since I've discussed these studies in detail in articles in *Bible Review* and *The Journal of Feminist Studies in Religion*, I won't go over them here. Suffice it to say that all of the arguments presented by Professor Trible today have been called into question, and few feminists remain as optimistic about the recoverability of this text as she is.[35]

New Developments

So, after 20 years of second-generation feminist investigations of the Bible, we seem to have followed the same path as our foresisters. We initially attempted to locate the patriarchy problem in interpretation. But the more work we did, the more evidence we found that pointed to the Bible itself. But just when the prospects of recovering a nonsexist, authoritative Bible were looking quite bleak, a new strategy appeared for shifting the problem out of the text.

In the 1970s and early 1980s, biblical scholarship in general was focused very much on the Bible as a literary text. More recently, scholarly interest has begun to move in the direction of focusing instead on the reader and the process of reading.

The scholarly question is no longer simply *what* the Bible means but *how* it means. Meaning, it is argued, involves more than decoding features of a text. It is a dynamic process of interaction between text and reader.

It was argued that every text has gaps or silences and that every author assumes readers bring some knowledge to their reading. Readers actually create new texts by combining their knowledge with what they encounter in the written text. This development in thinking seems to offer a new possibility to feminists who want to salvage the authority of the Bible. The strategy is to relocate meaning away from the text to the reader or the process of reading.

Mary Ann Tolbert, a feminist New Testament scholar thinks this strategy might be particularly useful to Protestant feminists. Because Protestantism made Scripture the sole religious authority, the idea of dropping any part of the Scriptures from the canon is unthinkable. At the same time, the Bible cannot be excused for its acts of "textual violence" against women on the grounds that it reflects past cultural norms. But if meaning is relocated in the reader rather than the text, then women can learn to read the Bible as women and exercise the freedom of making feminist readings authoritative rather than the text itself.[36]

A stronger articulation of this strategy is found in the work of Mary McClintock Fulkerson.[37] For Fulkerson, all meaning is a social signifying process—real meaning does not reside in texts and, therefore, cannot be gotten from texts. Instead, meaning is to be found in discursivity or the community of interpretation. So, if meaning is not a property of the text, then the Bible cannot be deemed sexist, and there is no direct correlation between the Bible and the oppression of women. According to Fulkerson, oppression is not an attribute of Scripture but a function of its being read.

There is part of this argument that I find attractive. I would certainly agree that meaning arises in the interaction between text and reader. But I am not willing to go as far as Fulkerson in shifting meaning from the text to the reader or to communities of interpretation. In my view, it is precisely because readers bring their own experiences and contexts to the reading process that multiple readings of any text produce multiple interpretations. However, if a text does not limit the semantic range in some way, then it hardly matters what text we use to produce meaning. If a text has no real meaning, if it cannot be sexist (or, presumably, racist, classist or anti-Semitic), then it should not matter whether we read the Bible, *Playboy* or Ku Klux Klan literature.

I am more persuaded by Mieke Bal's argument that both text and reader must be held accountable for meaning. For Bal, meaning is a readerly product but is rooted in the possibilities of the text. The text is the provider of meaning in the first moment, while in the second moment, "the reader formulates an ordering and reworking of the collection of possible meanings offered by the text."[38] Although Bal is decidedly not interested in the question of the authority of the Bible *per se*, she is interested in the ethical responsibility for and the political consequences of reading.

This brings me back to the work of David Clines. In his study of Song of Songs, Clines asked what effect reading such a text has on the reader, a question, he observes, that biblical scholars have rarely asked.[39] But it is a question that forces us to confront the issue of ethical responsibility and the politics of social power.

Until the rise of feminist criticism, readers of the Bible, or at least the community of interpretation, were almost exclusively male. We can discern the effects of the Bible on these readers by examining their commentaries. It is precisely because the biblical texts had the effects they did on male readers, and because of the social power of men in patriarchal societies, that women experienced the political consequences they did, consequences that ranged from being excluded from the public domain to being burned as witches. There is not a lot we can do about the past effects except document them, condemn them and work to see that they never happen again.

But what about the effect on readers today? Surely it makes a difference whether the reader is male or female, white or black, young or old, rich or poor. Such differences must account, at least in part, for the range of meanings produced by readers of the Bible.

When Clines puts this question to Song of Songs, he finds that most past readers read it not as a text about human love but as a text about the love of God for Israel or for the church. Allegorical or metaphorical interpretations were characteristic not only of celibate clerics prior to the Reformation, but also, and perhaps surprisingly, of Jewish and Protestant readers prior to the 19th century. He suggests, therefore, that the effect of this text on past male readers has been to produce interpretations involving a massive repression of sexuality. This, Clines asserts, is a testimonial to male fear of female sexuality and the refusal of male readers to come to terms with their own sexuality.

It seems apparent that Song of Songs has not had the effect of transforming power relations between the sexes in ancient Israel or in any society since then. And it is too late for it to have any major impact on contemporary social change because many other models for relations between the sexes now exist. But the male reader of today shares the male biblical author's perspective in a way that women readers do not. To the extent that the woman in the Song is the object of the male gaze, the text functions as a kind of soft pornography for men today in much the same way as it did for male readers in ancient Israel. At least that's what Clines argues.

The effect of a text like Judith may also be quite different on male and female readers. The message about the dangers of the *femme fatale* may largely be lost on women readers, while it may resonate with many other such messages men receive about the dangers of women and women's sexuality.

If we relocate meaning from the text to the reader or the reading process, does this alleviate the dilemma of biblical authority for Jewish and Christian feminists? Personally, I do not think so. It still leaves women reading the same male texts. We may have become much more sophisticated at being suspicious readers and at reading the text as women rather than adopting the male author's perspective. We may have become much more adept at constructing feminist meanings. But in my view, as long as we accord authoritative status to the biblical tradition, we accord authoritative status to patriarchy and sexist ideology.

Unlike our feminist sisters in other fields, we are not able to alter the canon by dropping some of the male texts and adding new women-authored texts. We are stuck with a collection within which women's voices have been virtually silenced and have to be teased out, if they can be found at all.

If we claim authoritative status for feminist readings, then we embroil ourselves in a power struggle with interpretive communities within which traditional patriarchal readings are normative, and there is, as yet, no compelling evidence to suggest that such a struggle can be won. Feminists have, after all, been working at this for 200 years, but the feminist view of the Bible is hardly normative in major Christian or Jewish denominations. Moreover, if we take this approach, we are still left with the problem that meaning is gendered. Men and women may construct very different meanings of the same text, meanings that arise from our differently gendered experiences. The *effect* of the reading process may, therefore, be quite different for men and women.

One of our principal feminist goals must be to ensure that the biblical text does not have the devastating effects on women's lives in the future that it has had in the past. I cannot see how shifting the locus of meaning and authority to the reader can accomplish this, short of teaching all men to read as women.

In my view, there is little in the recent work of feminist biblical scholars on this question of authority that eases the concerns of other feminists. At present we are witnessing attempts in many spheres to undo the recent social gains women have made. The malestream media and the religious right have done much to make feminism the f-word of the nineties. This is a time of so-called backlash or, more accurately, neosexism, and it is not difficult to find new examples of the Bible being used in the same old ways as a weapon against women.

There is a significant need for feminist critical analysis of the Bible and its effects on our society, but I doubt we will be perceived as serious feminist people as long as we try to fit the notion of an authoritative sacred canon into a feminist paradigm. The more important task, in my view, is to situate our work more centrally within the ongoing struggle for women's equality.

ENDNOTES

1. Gerda Lerner, *The Creation of Patriarchy* (Oxford: Oxford University Press, 1986), pp. 238–239; Chris Kramarae and Paula Treichler, *A Feminist Dictionary* (Boston: Pandora Press, 1985), pp. 323–324.

2. Lerner, *Creation of Patriarchy*, p. 240. Lerner proposes that sexism is to patriarchy as racism is to slavery.

3. David Clines, "What Does Eve Do to Help? And Other Irredeemably Androcentric Orientations in Genesis 1–3," *What Does Eve Do to Help? And Other Readerly Questions to the Old Testament*, Journal for the Study of the Old Testament Supplement Series (JSOTSup) 94 (Sheffield: JSOT Press, 1990), p. 45.

4. Randi Warne, "Toward a Brave New Paradigm: The Impact of Women's Studies on Religious Studies," *Religious Studies and Theology* 9:2 (1989), p. 35.

5. Lerner, *Creation of Patriarchy*, pp. 176–177.

6. Letty M. Russell, in the introduction to *Feminist Interpretations of the Bible*, ed. Russell (Philadelphia: Westminster Press, 1985), p. 14.

7. Eleanor Flexner, *Century of Struggle: The Women's Rights Movement in the United States*, rev. ed. (Cambridge, MA/London: Harvard University Press, Belknap Press, 1975), pp. 15–16.

8. Carolyn De Swarte Gifford, "American Women and the Bible: The Nature of Woman as a Hermeneutical Issue" in *Feminist Perspectives on Biblical Scholarship*, ed. Adela Yarbro Collins (Chico, CA: Scholars Press, 1985), pp. 12–13; Alice S. Rossi, ed., *The Feminist Papers: From Adams to de Beauvoir* (New York/London: Columbia University Press, 1973), p. 17.

9. Judith Sargent Murray, "On the Equality of the Sexes," as quoted in Rossi, *Feminist Papers*, p. 24.

10. Only Deuteronomy 4:32, 1 Chronicles 1:1 and Job 31:33 seem to allude to it.

11. For the history of interpretation of this text see Elaine Pagels, *Adam, Eve and the Serpent* (New York: Random House, 1988); John A. Phillips, *Eve: The History of an Idea* (San Francisco: Harper & Row, 1984); Bernard P. Prusak, "Woman: Seductive Siren and Source of Sin?" in *Religion and Sexism: Images of Women in Jewish and Christian Traditions*, ed. Rosemary R. Ruether (New York: Simon & Schuster, 1974).

12. Tertullian, "On the Apparel of Women," book 1, chap. 1, as quoted in *The Ante-Nicene Fathers: Translations of the Writings of the Fathers Down to A.D. 325*, ed. Alexander Roberts and James Donaldson (Grand Rapids, MI: Eerdmans, 1956), vol. 4, p. 14.

13. *Malleus Maleficarum* (1486), quoted in "The *Malleus Maleficarum*: The Woman as Witch" in *Women and Religion: A Feminist Sourcebook of Christian Thought*, ed. Elizabeth A. Clark and Herbert W. Richardson (New York: Harper & Row, 1977).

14. "The General Association of Massachusetts (Orthodox) to the Churches Under Their Care" in Rossi, *Feminist Papers*, pp. 305–306.

15. Margaret Hope Bacon, *Mothers of Feminism: The Story of Quaker Women in America* (San Francisco: Harper & Row, 1986), pp. 92–100; Gifford, "American Women and the Bible," pp. 14–15.

16. Sarah Grimké, "Letters on the Equality of the Sexes and the Condition of Women" in Rossi, *Feminist Papers*, pp. 306–318.

17. Miriam Gurko, *The Ladies of Seneca Falls: The Birth of the Women's Rights Movement* (New York: Schocken Books, 1974), pp. 9–10, 257.

18. Matilda Joslyn Gage, *Woman, Church and State: The Original Exposé of Male Collaboration Against the Female Sex* (1893; reprint, Watertown, MA: Persephone Press, 1980), pp. 237–238.

19. Elizabeth Cady Stanton, *The Woman's Bible* (1895–1898; reprint, Seattle: Coalition Task Force on Women and Religion, 1974), p. 214.

20. Gurko, *Ladies of Seneca Falls*, p. 286.

21. Ibid.

22. Gifford, "American Women and the Bible," pp. 28–30; Bacon, *Mothers of Feminism*, pp. 184–85; Clark and Richardson, *Women and Religion*, pp. 213–217.

23. Phyllis Trible, "Eve and Adam: Genesis 2–3 Reread" in *Womanspirit Rising: A Feminist Reader in Religion*, ed. Carol Christ and Judith Plaskow (New York: Harper & Row, 1979), p. 79.

24. Trible, "If the Bible's So Patriarchal, How Come I Love It?" *Bible Review* 8:5 (1992), p. 47.

25. Ibid.

26. Trible, "Postscript: Jottings on the Journey" in Russell, *Feminist Interpretations of the Bible*, p. 149.

27. See, for example, John Craghan, "Esther, Judith and Ruth: Paradigms for Human Liberation," *Biblical Theology Bulletin* 12 (1982), pp. 11–19, and "Judith Revisited," *Biblical Theology Bulletin* 12 (1982), pp. 50–53; Claudia Camp, "Woman Wisdom as Root Metaphor: A Theological Consideration" in *The Listening Heart: Essays on Wisdom and Psalms in Memory of Roland E. Murphy*, Kenneth G. Hoglund, Elizabeth Huwiler, J. Glass and Robert Lee, eds., JSOTSup 58 (Sheffield: Sheffield Academic Press, 1987), pp. 45–75.

28. Esther Fuchs, " 'For I Have the Way of Women': Deception, Gender, and Ideology in the Hebrew Bible," *Semeia* 42 (1988), pp. 68–83; "Who is Hiding the Truth? Deceptive Women and Biblical Androcentrism" in Collins, *Feminist Perspectives*, pp. 137–144.

29. Gale Yee, " 'I Have Perfumed My Bed With Myrrh': The Foreign Woman (*iššâ zārâ*) in Proverbs 1-9, JSOT 43 (1989), pp. 53-68.

30. Itumeleng J. Mosala, "The Implications of the Text of Esther for African Women's Struggle for Liberation in South Africa," *Semeia* 59 (1992), pp. 129–137.

31. Trible, *God and the Rhetoric of Sexuality* (Philadelphia: Fortress Press, 1978), p. 161.

32. Athalya Brenner, ed., *A Feminist Companion to the Song of Songs* (Sheffield: Sheffield Academic Press, 1993), pp. 28–29.

33. Clines, "Why Is There a Song of Songs? And What Does It Do to You If You Read It?" *Jian Dao* 1 (1994), pp. 3–27.

34. Pamela J. Milne, "What Shall We Do With Judith? A Feminist Reassessment of a Biblical 'Heroine' " *Semeia* 62 (1993), pp. 37–58.

35. David Jobling questions the whole notion that in a patriarchal society like ancient Israel anyone was capable of writing a story as feminist as Trible claims Genesis 2–3 to be. See David Jobling, "Myth and Its Limits in Genesis 2:4b–3:24" in *The Sense of Biblical Narrative: Structural Analyses in the Hebrew Bible 2*, JSOTSup 7 (Sheffield: JSOT Press, 1986), pp. 40–43.
I picked up on the structuralist work of Jobling and others to argue that even if we could learn to read the surface features of this text in a more woman-positive way the deep or mythic structures of the text convey a message of binary opposition, which has influenced centuries of misogynist interpretations and is likely to continue to do so. See Milne, "The Patriarchal Stamp of Scripture: The Implications of Structuralist Analysis for Feminist Hermeneutics," *Journal of Feminist Studies in Religion*, (JFSR) 5 (1989), pp. 17–34. David Clines examines Trible's interpretation of *ezer* (helper) and finds himself unable to support her feminist conclusions. The only task in which Eve helps is procreation, and this, too, seems to support patriarchal readings of the text. See Clines, "What Does Eve Do to Help?" pp. 25–48.
Susan Lanser challenges Trible's reading of *ha'adam* as a generic term. She points out that a reader infers masculine grammatical gender and sexual identity from the term because the text uses masculine pronouns with it and presents it as a human being. See Susan Lanser, "(Feminist) Criticism in the

Garden: Inferring Genesis 2–3," *Semeia* 41 (1988), pp. 67–84. Mieke Bal, although she agrees with some of Trible's arguments, emphatically rejects the idea that the story is either feminist or female-oriented. See Mieke Bal, "Sexuality, Sin, and Sorrow: The Emergence of the Female Character" in *Lethal Love: Feminist Literary Readings of Biblical Love Stories* (Bloomington, IN: Indiana University Press, 1987), pp. 104–130.

36. Mary Ann Tolbert, "Protestant Feminists and the Bible: On the Horns of a Dilemma" in *The Pleasure of Her Text: Feminist Readings of Biblical and Historical Texts,* ed. Alice Bach (Philadelphia: Trinity Press International, 1990), pp. 5–23.

37. Mary McClintock Fulkerson, "Contesting Feminist Canons: Discourse and the Problem of Sexist Texts," *JFSR* 7:2 (1991), pp. 53–73.

38. Mieke Bal, "Introduction," in *Anti-Covenant: Counter-Reading Women's Lives in the Hebrew Bible*, ed. Bal (Sheffield: Almond Press, 1989), pp. 11–24.

39. David Clines, "Why Is There a Song of Songs?" pp. 14–26.

*F*eminist questions about the New Testament are even more sensitive than about the Hebrew Bible. In the kind of comprehensive survey we're attempting today, a single speaker is going to cover the entire New Testament. You have already heard from Pam Milne about some of the things that have happened to Jane Schaberg because of her scholarly work on the New Testament. Perhaps part of this comes from the provocative nature of some of her titles. One was a book called The Illegitimacy of Jesus: A Feminist Theological Interpretation of the New Testament Infancy Narratives. I think I may have been responsible for the title of another article, "How Mary Magdalene Became a Whore," published in Bible Review.

The interesting thing is that this scholarly material—when you really evaluate it, it is indeed scholarly and not a diatribe—often enriches our understanding and appreciation of the biblical text, without destroying or denigrating faith or the text. Instead, it can deepen our understanding and enrich our faith.

Jane Schaberg received her Ph.D. at the place where Phyllis Trible now teaches, Union Theological Seminary in New York. Dr. Schaberg is professor of New Testament at the University of Detroit and has written several books and numerous scholarly articles. She will address us today on one of the most intriguing figures in the New Testament, Mary Magdalene. —H.S.

New Testament:
The Case of Mary Magdalene
❦
JANE SCHABERG

I would like to take this occasion to thank Hershel Shanks
for the tremendous work he's done in his publications.
First of all, he has made available to students and the educated public the discussions and debates of contemporary biblical scholarship. Second, he has placed these discussions in
the context of the visual arts through the centuries, thereby
constantly reminding us that these texts are works of art (whatever else they may be, and however flawed). I often think of the
line from Adrienne Rich that art can lie as well as tell the truth.

Third, he has put scholars in close dialogue with readers
who take the time to write letters (as with the old *MS.
Magazine*, the letters are sometimes the most interesting sec-
tions of *BAR* and *BR*). Fourth, he has given scholars the opportunity and challenge of speaking clearly, simply, in a nontech-
nical way, about their basic assumptions, methods, ideas and
results. This is extremely difficult to do in any field, and
extremely important. With this simplicity, we begin to see
more clearly fault lines, problems, shaky assumptions, as well
as the beauty and compelling quality of various interpretations
or approaches. Finally, I'd like to thank Hershel for his support
of feminist scholarship.

My work as a critic of the New Testament, or Second
Testament, differs in significant ways from the work of Hebrew
Bible, or First Testament, critics because the two testaments are
very different. In the Second Testament, we have 27 fairly short
books, which include a wide range of literary types—letters,

treatises, a sort of historical novel, an apocalypse, and four different accounts of the life, death and resurrection of Jesus of Nazareth. All of these works focus, in one way or another, on that one figure—on his teaching, the causes and meaning of his death, the impact of his life and the significance of belief in his resurrection on the communities that gathered in his name and memory.

We have a much tighter time frame for the production of these 27 works than for the production of the First Testament. The works that comprise the Second Testament were composed, most likely, within a hundred years of the death of Jesus. But not in the order that makes it easy to trace historical and theological developments—not first, that is, the accounts of Jesus and then of his impact. Instead, first we have seven or eight letters of Paul, plus a few attributed to him. Then we have the written accounts of Jesus' life and other writings. The stories of Jesus, moreover, are not eyewitness accounts to be taken at face value as reportage. They are careful compositions, interweaving and designing tradition and creativity in response to changing situations. Second Testament critics are interested in the history of the founder and the movement as well as in the final shape of the 27 documents and the ideas, beliefs and ideologies they present.

Another reason our work is different from that of Hebrew Bible scholars is that we live in a country or (speaking more widely) in a Western culture that, for some purposes, considers itself primarily Christian. We have to deal, in countries like the U.S., with Christian fundamentalism and its powerful backlash. All of us on this panel share the situation of working also within the backlash against feminism.

What I'd like to do today is look at some of the major problems and themes that interest feminist/womanist Second Testament scholars and at our invitation to question, challenge and answer these perplexing and powerful texts. A womanist is a black feminist or feminist of color; the term was coined by

Alice Walker[1] and defined by Delores S. Williams. Like white feminists, womanists affirm the full humanity of women but also "critique white feminist participation in the perpetuation of white supremacy, which continues to dehumanize black women."[2] Then I want to show how research on the figure of Mary Magdalene, a Gospel character, illustrates and focuses some of these concerns.

There are eight areas of feminist/womanist interest I would identify as major:

1. *The history* (as far as this can be constructed) of women in the early Christian movement. Work has been done on women in the Jesus movement during his lifetime and on women in the Pauline communities, especially at Corinth and Rome. Studies have been done on their prophetic and leadership roles and on what may have attracted them to the movement. This interest of ours shifts the focus away from the quest for the historical Jesus as an individualistic, unique male genius to the quest for a man and his close associates and their relationships to one another.

2. *Egalitarianism.* The egalitarian makeup and vision of that early movement is of great interest to feminists, as well as the gradual, subsequent patriarchalization of the movement, which is documented in even the earliest texts. This patriarchalization is evaluated as a tragic betrayal but one that is, hopefully, reversible today. Here I would say womanist thought in particular makes a profound contribution with its optimistic insistence that the egalitarian vision is still for everyone, for women and men, boys and girls.

3. *The Jewish context* of this movement and the egalitarianism of that context. This is a correction of an earlier trend in feminist New Testament scholarship, now recognized as "blaming the Jews for patriarchy," i.e., setting up the Jesus movement as feminist in sharp distinction to Judaism, which was wrongly imagined as monolithically sexist.

4. The living *images of women* in or derived from the Second Testament and how these images contribute to the shaping of gender ideals and roles, e.g., the Madonna Virgin-Mother; the sexual woman as a symbol of evil (the great whore of Babylon in Revelation, part of the long prophetic tradition that Pam mentioned); or women as silent, submissive, non-commissioned supporters of the movement who are nearly invisible in its communities.

5. *The Crucifixion and Resurrection.* Reexamination of how we understand the significance of Jesus' death, e.g., his death as a sacrificial atonement, especially when the understanding has fed into acceptance and glorification of suffering (of women, men, children, animals) and endorsed domination. I expect there will also be a feminist reexamination of the meaning of believing in resurrection. What are we to make of the element of embodiment, of the utopian vision drawn from apocalyptic literature?

6. *Canon.* Feminist scholars stress the need to go beyond the boundaries of canon, first to understand the canonical works in context and second to provide access to alternative religious visions. We want to trace the history of elements that later became marginal, experiments in community and leadership that were repudiated, and to uncover the contemporary relevance of the "roads not taken" by the so-called mainline church.

7. The fostering of *midrashic creativity.* Midrash, a rabbinic genre more than 1,500 years old, is an imaginative engagement with the biblical text, both with what *is* in the text and what is *not*, with what it offers and what it lacks, the ways it helps, the ways it hinders. Midrash can lead to recognition of the ambiguity and incompleteness and imperfection of the tradition as well a way of using one's own experience as a primary source of authority.

8. *The re-imagining of God.* An essential part of uncovering or constructing our history and voices is the theological project of conceiving of God/dess (as Ruether puts it) as a deity of all the people, a deity imagined by all, one that empowers all. In Second Testament studies, re-imagining God has taken the

form of speaking of God as a nonpatriarchal father (God's fatherhood cancels the patriarchal fatherhood of humans; "call no man father" is a saying of Jesus [Matthew 23:9]). Interest has also been focused on speaking of God as Sophia (Wisdom), the female figure found in Hebrew Bible wisdom literature and later apocrypha.

Each of these aspects of our current work expands and deepens our loyalties or, to put it another way, breaks the boundaries set by tradition, religious organizations, canon and convention. Now I'd like to look at the figure of Mary Magdalene from these eight angles.

1. *The history.* It takes some effort and concentration to separate what we know of the historical Mary Magdalene from the repentant whore of later legend. The historical Miriam of Migdal, a town on the western shore of the Sea of Galilee, was a member of the Jesus movement, probably in some leadership capacity (she is always named first among the women) and perhaps a source of financial support. In Luke 8:1-3 and Mark 16:9 (the Markan Appendix), we are told that she had been exorcised of seven demons—that is, she had been gravely ill and was healed.

All four Gospels of the Second Testament speak of her as following Jesus to Jerusalem, standing by at his crucifixion and burial and finding his empty tomb. Except in the Gospel of Luke, she is said to have been sent, alone or with other women, to tell the disciples that Jesus had been raised from the dead. According to three of the accounts (Matthew 28:9-10; John 20: 14-18; the Markan Appendix, Mark 16:9), she was the first one to whom the risen Jesus appeared.

If not for her, there might have been no Christian story. More than 150 years ago, David F. Strauss and Ernest Renan rightly considered her, after Jesus, the founder of Christianity, although they both attributed her belief in the resurrection of Jesus to near madness and romantic passion.[3]

2. *Egalitarianism.* Mary Magdalene's prominence (and the prominence of other women both in the Gospels and in the later communities) is a factor in the feminist discovery of and insistence on the egalitarian nature of the early Jesus movement. So too are the following factors: the absence of any sexist saying attributed to Jesus; his implicit criticism and subversion of patriarchy; his positive use of feminine symbols (such as the sweeping woman as the image of God); his open table fellowship with "sinners"; his reference to the Sophia of God and his understanding of himself as a prophet of Sophia.

But this is not a perfect proto-feminist picture. We have, to quote Judith Plaskow, "no evidence [that] Jesus was a champion of women's rights in the contemporary sense. He is never portrayed as arguing for women's prerogatives, demanding changes in particular restrictive laws that affect women or debating the Pharisees (or anyone else) on the subject of gender."[4] Nor is there an explicit description in the Gospels of women and men working together, although we have clear evidence from Paul of men and women as co-workers. So we may question, as Hisako Kinakawa does, whether or not real collaboration was ever realized in Jesus' lifetime.[5]

Another problematic bit of data about the historical Jesus is the probability that he chose 12 men to represent the eschatological dream of a restored Israel (Matthew 19:28; Luke 22:28–30), an image that eventually, as a result of Luke's concentration of authority in "the 12 apostles," helped to crowd women out of leadership roles.

Whatever life was actually like in the Jesus movement, and in spite of the important presence of women, the evidence shows that when events were recorded and remembered later, women's presence quickly began to be erased. There is no call narrative for Mary Magdalene (or any other woman) and no discussion or teaching during Jesus' ministry involving her. She is spoken to only by the figure(s) at the empty tomb and by the risen Jesus. Dialogue with her as an individual occurs only in the tomb scene in the Fourth Gospel. Her Easter witness is challenged by the male disciples, and in Mark 14:8 it is not even given, as she flees silent from the tomb.

Except in the Gospels, she is not mentioned in the Second Testament, not even in 1 Corinthians 15:5–8, where those who received resurrection appearances of Jesus authorizing and authenticating their leadership are listed. In Luke 24:34, as in 1 Corinthians 15:5, the first appearance is said to be to Peter (Cephas). John 20:8 presents the Beloved Disciple (a male whose name is not given) as the first one to believe.

Analyzing differences among the four canonical Gospel accounts of Jesus' crucifixion, empty tomb and post-resurrection appearances, we find that, as early as the Second Testament period, the powerful role of Mary Magdalene was in the process of being diminished and distorted. In the memories, traditions and rethinking of the Pauline and Lukan communities, her prominence was challenged by Peter; in Johannine circles, by the Beloved Disciple. Her partial effacement is related to the suppression of women's presence in the Epistles, which is also reflected in the household codes, which order the family in pyramidal, patriarchal fashion, and to commands that women be silent and subservient in the churches.

3. *Jewish Context.* Understanding the Jewish context of the egalitarianism of the Jesus movement (in that brief moment before it was squelched) means understanding that Jesus' acceptance of women and the strong presence of women in the movement represent "not a victory *over* early Judaism but a possibility *within* it."[6] Feminist studies of early Judaism (especially of epigraphical and archaeological evidence and nonrabbinic writings) indicate that *some* Jewish women may have been leaders in the synagogue and educated in Torah; they were also able to divorce their husbands, undertake business ventures, engage in prophetic, ecstatic activities, move around with comparative freedom and choose a communal lifestyle.

The historical Miriam of Migdal was a Jewish woman who was independent (her name is never associated with the name of a husband or son) and was linked with other Jewish women and men in a Jewish religious enterprise of historic significance. Participation required profound understanding and a creative grasp of Jewish traditions and possibilities, as well as courageous decisions to follow through in the face of Jesus' murder by the Roman government.

4. *Images of Women.* A fourth aspect of interest to feminist scholars is the patriarchal manipulation of images of women in order to reinforce setting up and maintaining social structures of inequality and domination. Patriarchal images of women were used to blame them, to warn them, to confine them, to undermine their self-confidence and talents, to wipe out their history and to idealize them. In short, they were used to hold them in a primary role as enablers of men.

The image of Mary Magdalene is a fascinating example of this manipulation. In spite of the Second Testament evidence we have discussed, the word most people free-associate with her is "whore." She is the repentant whore, the whore who loved and was forgiven by Jesus. This image often reappears today, from a song in Whoopie Goldberg's *Sister Act* to Scorcese's *The Last Temptation of Christ* to Andrew Lloyd Weber and Tim Rice's "Jesus Christ Superstar." Once you notice it, you begin to see it everywhere. The image now has a nearly 2,000-year history in legend and art.

How did Mary Magdalene, who is mentioned by name only in the texts discussed above, become a whore? By the post-Second Testament conflation, or blending and tangling, of texts that mention her with texts that do not. Especially there is conflation with the highly artistic and memorable scene in Luke 7 where the sinful "woman in the city" interrupts a meal at the house of a Pharisee, where Jesus is a guest, and, weeping, bathes his feet with her tears, dries them with her hair, kisses them and anoints them.[7] This woman's actions are interpreted as a living parable of love resulting from and leading to forgiveness. Whereas the Second Testament accounts of Mary Magdalene are silent about her background and motivation, Luke 7, a text that has nothing to do with her, provides a background (prostitution) and motivation (love grateful for forgiveness, shading into romantic love) for Mary Magdalene, which became the dominant facets of our memory of her. The conflation began as early as the second or third century C.E.

Legends associated mainly with Provence in southern France provide a post-Gospel life for the Magdalene. In one strand, she spends the end of her life, 30 solitary years, in dramatic repentance in the dank, dripping grotto of Saint Baume, a high cave inaccessible to everyone but angels and people with very strong hiking shoes. In the post-Reformation period, when the Roman church stressed the sacrament of penance, the ascetic, weeping Magdalene was a popular instrument of propaganda. In thousands of artistic depictions of her, her past life as a whore was not forgotten but was crudely signaled by complete or partial nudity and provocative Playmate-like poses of "pious pornography."[8]

She became the patron saint of prostitutes, called Magdalenes. Portraits of mistresses and wives posing as the Magdalene were commissioned. Take a tour through any major art museum, and you can follow her histrionic, voluptuous, beautiful images and ponder the distance between them and her shadowy Gospel figure. The distortion of her image, Elisabeth Schüssler Fiorenza has remarked, shows the deep distortion in the attitudes toward, and in the self-understanding and identity of, Christian women and men.[9]

The Magdalene of legend and art is woman reduced to wild sexuality, which must be punished, woman supposedly fully explained by romantic love. She is a male fantasy. At root, these legends are a reaction against her power and authority as the major Christian witness, which they obscure. By thinking back to the historical figure, women can begin to reassert control of our religious models and thus of our religious lives.

5. *The Crucifixion and Resurrection.* A fifth area of feminist interest is the meaning of Jesus' crucifixion and resurrection. One of the characters in a book by mystery writer P. D. James calls the cross the "stigma of the barbarism of officialdom and of man's ineluctable cruelty."[10] Womanist scholars have been especially trenchant in their criticism of the acceptance and glorification of suffering and sacrifice that is part of Christian theology. Delores S. Williams, for example, writes, "There is nothing divine in the blood of the cross...[which] only represents historical evil trying to defeat good." Redemption, Williams argues, comes not through Jesus' death but through his ministerial vision of righting relationships, his life of resistance.[11]

We have, as far as we know, no record of the thoughts or impressions of the women at the cross of Jesus. I like to think their reactions were similar to the reactions of the protagonist in Margaret Atwood's 1972 novel, *Surfacing,* when she comes upon a dead heron strung up on a tree, an act of meaningless "American" cruelty. To her, the heron is a sacred object, like Christ to the Christian. She identifies with the heron but also feels a "sickening complicity, sticky as glue, blood on my hands, as though I had been there and watched without saying no or doing anything to stop it."[12] As she comes to self-awareness, she divorces herself from the interpretations men use to justify their crimes.[13] She understands the life power rising from death, and she proclaims: "This above all, to refuse to be a victim...[to] give up the old belief that I am powerless." Eventually, that is, she begins to say no. Quite a different reaction than, say, Paul or Luke's to the cross of Christ![14]

We do have vestiges of the witness of women associated with the empty tomb. This tradition, which appears in all the canonical Gospels as well as the Gospel of Peter, is not much in favor with many male historical Jesus scholars, such as Crossan,[15] Mack[16] and Borg.[17] They view the tradition of the empty tomb as a late historical addition and associate it with a crass understanding of resurrection, primarily because of the inherent assumption that it matters what happened to the *corpse*, as opposed to the *spirit*, of Jesus.

Feminist scholars are re-examining those assumptions of lateness and crassness. They are raising the question of how the testimony of women about the empty tomb and "appearances" to them (revelations) fit into the schema of development of the Easter faith. How are we to understand the empty tomb tradition ("he is not here"; the corpse is not here) in the light of Jewish apocalyptic expectations and the feminist interest in embodiment? How and why does it matter what happened to the corpse of Jesus?[18]

6. *Canon.* A study of the Magdalene in noncanonical documents of the first four centuries C.E. shows the importance of breaking out of the canon. Magdalene appears in several Gnostic writings, such as the Gospel of Thomas, the Gospel of Philip, Sophia of Jesus Christ, Dialogue of the Savior, Pistis Sophia and the Gospel of Mary (Magdalene). These works preserve and develop a tradition of her authority and the jealous rivalry or conflict between her and Peter and other male disciples. In the Gnostic tradition, when she is challenged, the Savior (or, once, Levi) defends her. Neither silenced nor excluded, she speaks out boldly and powerfully, entering into long dialogues with the risen Jesus and comforting, correcting and encouraging his male disciples. In these works she is a visionary, a spiritual guide and teacher praised for her understanding and often identified as the intimate "companion" of the Savior.

Unlike the Mary Magdalene of later Western legend and art, the Gnostic Magdalene is not, and was not, a prostitute or sinner. She does not represent repentance or forgiveness or chastised sexuality. Nor is she the Savior's romantic or sexual partner, his favorite woman.[19] Rather, the erotic element, which is present in the Gnostic works (Jesus is said to have kissed her and preferred her), appears to indicate a mystical communion. Love is based on her intellectual and spiritual grasp of the Savior's teachings.

Mary Magdalene functioned in Gnostic circles both as a representative of the female followers of Jesus and as a symbol of the importance and leadership of women among the Gnostics. She may have been a prophetic role model, on whose memory women in some circles, for a time, based their successful claims to power. The hypothesis that she reflects the prominent roles women *actually played* in these communities as leaders and as sources of revelation and authority is difficult to test but is, nevertheless, in the process of being tested. Thanks in great part to the ongoing analysis of Gnostic materials, we can now glimpse the tradition that was displaced, distorted, lost and overlaid by the legend of Mary Magdalene the whore.

We can glimpse the early Christian arguments in favor of women's leadership, allowing us to see that views excluding women were only one side of a hotly debated issue. As Karen King notes, the exclusion from the canon, under the label of heresy, of "every significant type of early Christianity which supported women's leadership" is a fact that we cannot ignore. "To raise the issue of canonical authority," she writes, "means asking why these traditions have been labeled as wrong ('heretical'), and how the canon became closed." The "heresy" involved understanding "inspiration" as ongoing, as dwelling among people rather than in texts, and of prophetic experience as the basis of spiritual authority.[20] This leads also to a reevaluation of "heresy."

7. *Midrashic Creativity.* Women and men, in offices, workshops, study groups, classrooms and even churches and synagogues in many countries, are creating midrash off the springboard of the canonical texts.[21] Let me mention particularly the feminist midrash of Alicia Suskin Ostriker, *Feminist Revision and the Bible,* and her new book that's just come out, *The Nakedness of the Fathers: Biblical Visions and Revisions.*

The Magdalene material (canonical and noncanonical, legendary and artistic) is interesting stuff to work with in this regard. Focus for a minute on biblical intertextuality, which involves such ventures as these. One might ask oneself or one's students to:

- rewrite the ending of the Gospel of Mark (which ends with the women fleeing the empty tomb in fear and silence)
- write an ending to Mark that might have been suppressed by some early Christians
- imagine the on-the-road experiences of women in the Jesus movement
- name and get rid of the seven demons of the Magdalene
- express the thoughts of the Magdalene at the cross
- create a dialogue between the historical Magdalene and the unnamed woman in Luke 7 or the Magdalene's repentant prostitute legendary self or her images in the art museums

These imaginative exercises require tapping into your own anger and hope and power, your own experiences. In contrast to the deformed images of Magdalene, feminist midrash is an attempt to find a different Magdalene, to chart a steady course between the shoals of romantic love and penitential grovelling.

This Mary Magdalene will not moan about her past whoring and will not be defined by her sexual attractiveness. She will be a woman redeemed but not rendered sexless,[22] a mystic and a thinker. She will have new things to say, especially if her class or race is imagined in different ways, as when Alicia Suskin Ostriker imagines Lilith as a black woman.[23] In the absence of historical information about Mary Magdalene, we can follow a different trajectory. Rather than drawing her image from the Second Testament texts conventionally associated with her (the "sinner" in Luke 7, the woman taken in adultery in John 8, the silent, contemplative Mary of Bethany at the feet of Jesus in Luke 10), we can draw instead on the story of the unnamed woman in Mark 14, whose anointing of Jesus is a prophetic act of power.[24]

8. *Re-imagining God.* The re-imagined God of the re-imagined and reconstructed Mary Magdalene is quite different from the God said to have dishonored Miriam in the Hebrew

Bible (like a father spitting in his daughter's face), the God who sent Hagar back into slavery or the God who remained silent at the abandonment of Tamar, the Levite's concubine and Jephthah's daughter, different from the God thought to countenance the silencing of women prophets, the covering of women's heads, the subservience of women to men (e.g., 1 Timothy 2:8–15). The God whom feminist scholars are teaching us to re-imagine as Sophia (Wisdom) sends women prophets as well as men, stands by them, is justified by them, notices and remembers when their blood is shed (Luke 7:35; Matthew 18:34–36).

In the wake of the return of the goddesses, to use Tikva's phrase, we are in the midst of a profound change in cultural consciousness, a new understanding of the feminine in relation to the divine. Feminist thought represents this transformation in consciousness, which demands the transformation of social forms and modes of action and responds to them. The aim, as the motto of the journal *Feminist Studies* puts it, is "not just to interpret women's experiences but to change women's condition." This means dissolving old loyalties, in terms of our conversation here, loyalties to canon (sacred texts), doctrine, orthodoxy, gender roles, versions of history, understanding of authority, exclusive communities and even religions.

Virginia Woolf called "freedom from unreal loyalties" a great teacher[25] of women. Once women, she wrote, have some wealth, some knowledge, and some service to *real* loyalties, they "can enter the professions and escape the risks that make them undesirable." Elsewhere she wrote, "As a woman, I have no country."[26] As women we also have no religion. Or the religion we do have is considered heresy, as males define it.[27]

Feminist scholarly work on the figure of Mary Magdalene is restoring the historical figure and her potential to inspire, instruct and energize. This work is aided by 20th-century methodologies and discoveries like the Gnostic documents from Nag Hammadi. But we have also found, with regard to the Bible as well as other subjects, that Foucault was right when he said society does not suddenly discover or rediscover truth, for example, the truth that Mary Magdalene was a leader, not a whore. Changes in politics govern what is accepted as truth. In other words, something is shifting in the relations of power.[28] Our very presence here on this panel illustrates this shift.

ENDNOTES

1. Alice Walker, *In Search of Our Mothers' Gardens* (San Diego: Harcourt Brace Jovanovich, 1983), p. xi.

2. Delores S. Williams, *Sisters in the Wilderness* (Maryknoll, NY: Orbis Books, 1993), p. xiv.

3. See Susan Haskins, *Mary Magdalene: Myth and Metaphor* (London: HarperCollins, 1993), pp. 330–331.

4. Judith Plaskow, "Anti-Judaism in Feminist Christian Interpretation" in *Searching the Scriptures*, vol. 1, ed. Elisabeth Schüssler Fiorenza (New York: Crossroad, 1993), p. 119.

5. See Hisako Kinakawa, *Women and Jesus in Mark* (Maryknoll, NY: Orbis Books, 1994), p. 91.

6. Plaskow, "Anti-Judaism," p. 124.

7. I want to stress that this conflation of stories and persons is *not* done by the Gospel writers and is *not* found in the Second Testament Gospels.

8. Haskins, *Mary Magdalene*, p. 265. See also Marjorie M. Malvern, *Venus in Sackcloth* (Carbondale, IL: Southern Illinois University Press, 1975).

9. Schüssler Fiorenza, "Mary Magdalene: Apostle to the Apostles," *Union Theological Seminary Journal* (April 1975), p. 5.

10. P.D. James, *The Children of Men* (New York: Alfred A. Knopf, Inc., 1993), p. 50.

11. See Williams, *Sisters in the Wilderness*, pp. 167, 165. On sacrificial ritual as enacting patrilineal descent, a "remedy for having been born of woman" and "birth done better," see Nancy Jay, *Throughout Your Generations Forever* (Chicago: University of Chicago Press, 1992). Asking why, throughout the world, women can not and do not sacrifice while men voluntarily shed blood in sacrifice, Jay sees sacrifice as "establishing bonds of intergenerational continuity between males that transcend their absolute dependence on childbearing women" (p. 147), in other words, a means of disempowering women.

12. Margaret Atwood, *Surfacing* (New York: Simon & Schuster, 1972), p. 150.

13. Carol Christ, *Diving Deep and Surfacing* (Boston: Beacon Press, 1980), p. 46.

14. See Karen King, "The Gospel of Mary [Magdalene]" in *Searching the Scriptures*, vol. 2, ed. Schüssler Fiorenza (New York: Crossroad, 1994), p. 610. In the Gospel of Mary, the disciples who think following the Savior will lead to suffering have completely misunderstood: "the Savior's intention is to lead them away from suffering and death." In this work, attachment to the body is the source of suffering and death, and one must overcome that attachment: "there is no promise of, or desire for a physical resurrection." Jesus' death is real (no docetism) and so is the possibility of persecution; but "neither Jesus' death nor martyrdom is invested with salvific meaning. The Savior came to alleviate suffering, not to chart a path to salvation by bringing it upon his disciples."

15. See Crossan's response to the following comment, which was made at a symposium on the search for the historical Jesus at the Smithsonian Institution in 1993. "I think," said the questioner, "you have enunciated a male point of view. It was Mary Magdalene who got to the tomb first, and she was the first person to recognize Jesus." Crossan replied that the ending of the Gospel of Mark (where the women run away and tell no one) is part of Mark's polemic against the family and disciples of Jesus, and he doesn't "put much on that, in itself." As for John 20, as John depicts the Magdalene "she keeps getting it wrong" when she repeats that the body has been stolen. She is an important leader being downgraded by the Johannine community. Crossan says, if one "wanted to find a woman to exalt" [*sic*] or "an ideal female Christian hero," the unnamed woman who anoints Jesus in Mark 14:3–9 should be "claimed" (*The Search for Jesus: Modern Scholarship Looks at the Gospels*, ed. Hershel Shanks [Washington, DC: Biblical Archaeology Society, 1993], pp. 127–128).

16. Burton L. Mack, *A Myth of Innocence* (Philadelphia: Scholars Press, 1991), pp. 88, 96, 237–238.

17. E.g., "I doubt that there was an empty tomb. I doubt that anything happened to Jesus' corpse. But...whether there was an empty tomb or whether anything happened to the corpse of Jesus has nothing to do with the truth of Easter. The truth of Easter is grounded in the ongoing experience of Jesus as a living reality in the lives of Christians" (Marcus J. Borg, reply to letter, *Bible Review* 10:4 [1994], pp. 47–48).

18. I'm thinking here of Karen King's remark that the Gnostic belief in the relative lack of value of the material world could be used to support the hegemonic interests of the upper class. "Such belief can leave intact exploitative economic and class structures by turning attention away from the world to spiritual matters" ("Gospel of Mary [Magdalene]," in Shüssler Fiorenza, *Searching the Scriptures*, vol. 2, p. 624). What other forms of the Easter faith function this way?

19. See David Curzon, "A Hidden Genre: Twentieth-Century Midrashic Poetry," *Tikkun* 9 (1994), pp. 70–71, 95. For feminist midrash, Alicia Suskin Ostriker, *Feminist Revision and the Bible* (Oxford: Blackwell, 1993), and *The Nakedness of the Fathers: Biblical Visions and Revisions* (New Brunswick, NJ: Rutgers University Press, 1994).
See also Gerda Lerner, *The Creation of Feminist Consciousness* (New York: Oxford University Press, 1993), p. 190, on how Emily Dickinson transformed the common language of biblical metaphor, Christian myth and poetic reference, giving them her own meanings without respect to an "institutional framework of explanation" from Church or traditional theology. Lerner stresses that "women's auton-

omy had to be hard-won before creativity could flourish" (p. 179). She describes how women like Dickinson authorized themselves and empowered themselves to think and speak by relying on their own creative talent. "These were the innovators who simply by-passed patriarchal thought and created alternate worlds" (p. 19).

20. See Haskins, *Mary Magdalene*, p. 144.

21. See King, "Gospel of Mary [Magdalene]": Mary is not merely the Savior's favorite female, as Peter would have it; she is his most favored disciple (p. 616; n.13, p. 630).

22. Ibid.

23. See Ostriker's presentation of Lilith: "I am the woman with hair in a rainbow/Rag, body of iron/I take your laundry in, suckle your young/scrub your toilets/...I am the one you confess/Sympathy for, you are doing a study/Of crime in my environment, of rats/In my apartment, of my/Sexual victimization, you're raising money/To send my child to summer camp, you'd love/If I were not so sullen/And so mute" ("Lilith to Eve: House, Garden" in *Feminist Revision and the Bible*, pp. 92–93). See also "Lilith Unveils Herself": "You feel me squeeze between you and the man/I hug your body, girl, I breathe/*Have courage*" (p. 96).

24. The identification of these two characters would be more plausible historically (the woman who recognizes and points out Jesus as Messiah has the guts to stand at the cross and return to the tomb). The woman who anoints Jesus before his death, however, is named Mary of Bethany in the Fourth Gospel.

25. "[F]reedom from loyalty to old schools, old colleges, old churches, old ceremonies, old countries...freedom from pride of nationality, religious pride, college pride, school pride, family pride, sex pride and those unreal loyalties that spring from them." The other teachers are poverty (having enough money to be independent), chastity (refusal to sell your brain) and derision (flinging back honors; preferring for psychological reasons obscurity, censure and ridicule) (Virginia Woolf, *Three Guineas* [London: Harcourt Brace Jovanovich, (1938)], pp. 78–80).

26. Ibid.

27. See Ross Shepard Kraemer's chapter, "Heresy as Women's Religion: Women's Religion as Heresy" in *Her Share of the Blessings* (New York: Oxford University Press, 1992). We are learning to value our "heretics," such as Simone Weil, Emily Dickinson, Etty Hillesum and Sor Juana de la Cruz.

28. See Michel Foucault, "Truth and Power" in *The Foucault Reader*, ed. Paul Rabinow (New York: Pantheon Books, 1984): "Truth isn't outside power, or lacking in power...Truth is a thing of this world" (p. 72). " 'Truth' is linked in a circular relation with systems of power which produce and sustain it, and to effects of power which it induces and which extends it....The problem is not changing people's consciousnesses—or what's in their heads—but the political, economic, institutional regime of the production of truth...of detaching the power of truth from the forms of hegemony, social, economic, and cultural, which it operates at the present time" (pp. 74–75). See also Jay (*Throughout*, p. 147): "what feminist theory illuminates has not been hidden but only ignored, has not been invisible but only irrelevant"; and Gloria Albrecht, *The Character of Our Communities* (Nashville: Abingdon Press, forthcoming).

Panel Discussion

❦

HERSHEL SHANKS: There's someone who hasn't been heard from yet, and we're going to give that someone a chance now. You've been silent all day. Stretch for three minutes, and then you can fire away at us.

I'd like to ask a question that has three parts. First, how did I get the impression the Canaanites really practiced a fertility cult? And second, what about the Israelites? What were the prophets so exercised about? Third, what did the frequent references to the high places mean?

TIKVA FRYMER-KENSKY: The story of how we developed the notion of an orgiastic Canaanite religion is fascinating and has been documented rather well in a book called *The Bible Without Theology*, by Robert A. Oden, Jr. Oden shows quite clearly the leaf that was taken from Herodotus. But on this matter, Herodotus is extremely biased and unreliable. He reports that once in the lifetime of every woman of Babylon she had to serve the goddess Mellita, whom he calls Ishtar Mellita, by being a sacred prostitute (a *Qedesha*). She had to go to the courtyard of the temple and sit on the ground until a man propositioned her. She was not allowed to haggle about the price but had to accept whatever was offered, sleep with him, and give the money to Ishtar. Then she was freed of the service and could go home. Herodotus adds that women who did this when they were young and nubile got rid of the obligation in short order. But if they waited too long, they could sit around for four years. (Laughter.)

As you can imagine, this story struck the fancy of classical historians, most of whom quote Herodotus without attribution and just repeat it. When critical biblical scholarship really got going at the end of the 19th century, this orgiastic *rite de passage* was moved, in a breath, from Babylon to Canaan and became a new mythology of what Canaanite religion was like.

Now partly this reflects the fevered sexual imagination of repressed scholars. (Laughter.) But partly it is more serious and involved with the process of patriarchalization. Patriarchy has a tendency to exclude or denigrate whatever it doesn't like by sexualizing it. We use words like "whore" and "bitch" as terms of derogation. We use words that refer to copulation as slang terms for doing somebody a dirty deed.

With that kind of mentality, it became almost inevitable that the religion the prophets railed against look more sexual, in particular through the metaphor of females out of control. Take the metaphor of Judah spreading her legs under every tree and on the high places (Jeremiah 2–3, for example). It's not the women of Judah who are doing this. The passages actually refer to the state signing a political alliance with Egypt, which means, in effect, finding a master other than God and, therefore, fornicating. This is simply another example of the tendency to sexualize what we do not like. Putting it all together, this led to a lively mythology about the high places and what the Canaanites were doing there.

One more thing should be mentioned. The high places and the cult that was practiced there were part and parcel of Israel's old-time religion. During the prophetic movement, it coincides with the monarchic tendency to control and centralize religious observance. After all, Samuel, in the days before the monarchy, officiated at a high place. By the time of Hosea, however, Hosea no longer likes the high places. He's kind of a proto-Deuteronomist who supports central control. By the time of Jeremiah, the idea that there are places of worship other than the Temple has become very, very disturbing.

We see the same process in graphic images, like the grand serpent that, according to legend, Moses made. This serpent is kept in the Temple until it is destroyed by Hezekiah (2 Kings 18:4) as something foreign to the Israelite religion. As biblical monotheism grows and develops, whatever is jettisoned is labeled foreign, Canaanite and vaguely sexy, in the bad sense, somehow too hot to handle.

This mythology is what led to our writing history as if the Israelites emerged from the desert with a pure faith and came to the wicked cities of Canaan, where they learned all bad things. In truth, the religion of Israel is the product of continual questioning and questing for God, a response to God's mandate, a constant reexamination of the past to see what fits into the religious sensibility of the present.

That continual transformation eventually led to the abandonment of the high places and images like the Nechushtan (the snake [2 Kings 18:4]) and the practices of the *Qedeshot*. The only glimpse we have of what the *Qedeshot*, sometimes translated as sacred prostitutes, actually did in the Temple is that when Josiah kicks them out he closes off the room where they sat weaving garments (2 Kings 23:7). How that turns into ladies who bed for hire, I do not know. (Applause.)

This is a question for Miss Milne. Does your rejection of the Bible as hopelessly patriarchal mean that you deny the Bible has any spiritual authority for feminists? Does it mean feminists of faith have to start from scratch to work out their relationship with God?

PAMELA J. MILNE: I think I'd have to say no, it doesn't mean that someone can't draw spiritual nourishment from the Bible. But I would prefer that they didn't try to do that. The reason I say that is because I think it is time for a more social and less individualistic approach to the Bible. The way I understand positions such as Professor Trible's and Professor Frymer-Kensky's (not what we heard today in the discussion by

Professor Frymer-Kensky, but from my personal discussions with her) is that the Bible does something for them as individuals. I would like us to think about women as a social group.

Now maybe this reflects a difference between the way Canadians and Americans think. (Laughter.) In the United States, there is a tremendous emphasis on individuals, on individual rights, on protecting individuals and thinking in terms of individuals, whereas in Canada we tend to think more in terms of group rights. So maybe I have a more social point of view.

For me, drawing personal or individual spiritual sustenance from a text like this does not compare in importance with the damage the Bible has done to women as a social group. In other words, by continuing to give individual or personal validity to this text—because it gives you religious sustenance or because it is religiously authoritative in your life—you may contribute to the ongoing social oppression that has been so problematic for women and continues to this day.

So my preference would be that we think on a bigger scale. If it comes to a choice between dropping or denying authority to a text such as the Bible, on the one hand, or taking care of myself, my own spiritual needs, on the other hand, I would opt for the group, for the social rather than the individual concern.

I'm not denying that feminists *can* find spiritual value in the text as a result of their ability to read it the way they choose. But when we move from the individual feminist perspective to conventional social uses of the Bible, I have concerns. I would prefer to see feminists leave it behind. I completely agree with Professor Frymer-Kensky that going back and reclaiming the goddess traditions from Mesopotamia as a starting point for new feminist spirituality is not where it's at. I can't see any point in spending time doing that.

I have suggested in some of my writing the kind of strategy you heard a bit about from Professor Schaberg. You can also find it in the writings of women such as Mieke Bal. To some extent these feminist scholars look at women's writings and, at the very least, juxtapose expressions of women's religious experiences to texts like the Bible. Personally, I'd like woman-positive texts to replace the Bible. But at a minimum, we have to get women's religious experiences in there in a way they have not gotten in there by limiting ourselves to the biblical text.

FRYMER-KENSKY: I want to jump into this discussion for a moment. The key words are "authoritative text" and "authority." The Bible, when we study it in its original context and language and intertextually and with all the modern techniques, is an extremely complex document that revels in a multiplicity of voices, that is filled with gapped texts, that demands that the interpreter complete the text, that raises all kinds of significant issues, that critiques its own society and confesses its divided opinion about everything. The Bible is a document of struggle, of God-wrestling. It is the record of a society and the response of individuals who constantly go back over their history and think about these things.

Most of this is obscured by our religious traditions, which have simplified the stories and the text and distilled particular messages from it and used them to bludgeon people, especially women, but others as well, into a vision of an orderly world with a hierarchic system and vision of power. But it's important to listen to the Bible's own words—the mandate to seek justice, the mandate to be holy—and to the description, at its best, of a God who is just and merciful and gracious and people loving. We should take every story and every idea presented through interpretation as authoritative and submit it to this simple test—is this justice as I have been taught by the Bible and my religious tradition to understand it? Are people being treated as completely human? Does this lead to a holy society in which everybody is valued as being made in the image of God?

When we learn to do that—and not simply accept the authority either of our religious leaders or of traditional interpretations, or even of the written word itself, but to keep this dynamic process going—then we're into true spiritual nourishment, nourishment for our communities as well as for us as individuals. Then the Bible can serve as a nourishing factor. But the more it is used as a proof-text and a bludgeon, the more it is forced into constrictive modes of life-denying interpretation, the less valuable it is. (Applause.)

JANE SCHABERG: I want to say a word about the notion mentioned by Professor Milne of replacing the Bible. I think you disempower Margaret Atwood's image, and other images like hers, if you think in terms of replacing the Bible. Atwood doesn't mean to replace the Bible. She means the hanged heron to draw on the image of the crucified innocent one. I like to think of a slide over a slide, a transparency over a transparency, rather than replacing one image with another. We need the tradition, the aspects of the prophetic tradition and aspects of the Christian tradition that empower resistance to domination.

MILNE: I'd like to make one last comment. My concerns are really pragmatic. One of the difficulties we face now is illiteracy. When I go into the classroom, I'm faced with students who have difficulty reading the written text. They have not grown up reading and writing. They've grown up watching TV and listening to tapes and CDs.

Unlike some of the other panelists, I don't teach in a religious institution. Like Professor Schaberg, I don't teach theological students primarily. I teach in a provincial university, so I get ordinary students off the street. And most of them have never cracked the Bible. They may sign up for a Bible course, but only about 10 percent of them are familiar with the Bible. To think that they are going to become literate enough to read the Bible with the sophistication needed for feminist reinterpretations takes more optimism than I have.

I think most people today encounter the biblical tradition through other means—through TV preachers (mostly fundamentalist), through movies, through musicals. They don't, for the most part, encounter it in the traditional way of opening the book and reading it. They might read little bits of it in a church context, if they still go. But Bible literacy is on the decline. So, for me, the problem is overwhelming. I just don't know how the transformation of understanding along the lines suggested by feminist reformists can be accomplished.

S H A N K S :   You're making a kind of a political decision, aren't you, Pam? You don't deny that women can draw rich spiritual nourishment from the Bible, when read sensitively, the way Phyllis Trible or Tikva would read it. I wonder, if you were to apply the same tests that you apply to the Bible, if you wouldn't have to throw out all ancient literature. As we heard from Tikva, they were all patriarchal societies, and we were, too, until very recently. As a matter of fact, as you pointed out to me at lunch, we still are. (Laughter.) So we would almost have to throw out everything.

Tikva has spent much of her scholarly career studying clay tablets, which are so unattractive with those little chicken-scratchings on them. And yet she has taken those texts, like any mythology (even if you want to denigrate the biblical text as pure mythology), she has taken them and found richness in them. Are you saying that, because of the political problem, because we can't separate the Bible from the powers that be who use it to suppress women, that we should discard it as irrelevant, even though we can find spiritual nourishment in it?

M I L N E :   No, I think I made my position clear. I don't think we can discard the Bible because it pervades our culture in so many ways. I mean, we can't even buy some computers without coming in contact with the image of Genesis 2–3. It's planted right on the front of the computer. (Laughter.)

There's so much in our society that we can't understand or deal with without being in contact with the Bible in some way. And there are many important things in ancient literatures, including the Bible, such as the reconstruction of women's lives in history. We know women weren't absent from history. Most of our written records just don't talk about them very much.

From a feminist point of view, the process I see going on with feminists who take a historical approach, which I think is perfectly legitimate academically, is very much needed. In that sense, I'm not advocating throwing out the Bible. It's an important historical document. It's an important literary document, too, and can be studied purely as a literary document.

SHANKS: How about as a spiritual document?

MILNE: I think the dangers the Bible poses outweigh tne benefits. That is not to say that individual women cannot derive spiritual value from it. Clearly, two, perhaps three, of the people on this panel do. But my concern is how to minimize the negative consequences if you're going to accord the Bible some kind of authoritative status.

When Phyllis was talking about teasing elements out of the text, these bits about Miriam, I thought to myself, if we took this book out into the streets of this city and asked people to read this or that text, what are the chances they would see these things on their own? It takes great literary insight to find these kinds of things in this text. Realistically, how successful can we be in teaching an entire society to use it this way, to find those messages in it? People are becoming less connected to the biblical tradition rather than more connected to it.

TRIBLE: I'd like to say a couple of things. So-called people on the street, or laypeople, come up with all kinds of surprising readings of the text. They play hunches that scholars may never have dreamt of. The scholar may think that she has teased something out, but later she learns that a particular Bible study group in a particular church always thought that was the case anyway. (Chuckles.) So the lines get blurred. The Southern Baptist missionary I spoke of was not a theologian educated in biblical studies. In fact, scholars would have told her at the time that she was way off the wall for saying that woman was created last and was, therefore, the best.

Let me also put in a word for communities of faith who are studying the Bible and, in particular, groups of women within churches and synagogues who have been banding together for years and years now and for the difference they have made in those denominations and in the larger arena.

Also, let me put in a word for crossing the lines between Judaism and Christianity. Tikva and I met years ago at the University of Michigan when I was out there speaking, and she was a respondent. Something caught fire between us, and over the years we have continued our conversation. We have also shared participation in communities of faith within our own religions. And we have a dream. I guess now it has to be an eschatological vision (Laughter.)—that one day the two of us will write a little book we've long talked about called *Feminists Who Love the Bible*. It would have a double authorship, and it would cross the line between Judaism and Christianity. (Applause.)

SCHABERG: I would like to respond to this issue of social readings and individualistic readings. In Detroit we are privileged to have a large African American community. God knows, if any group has been oppressed by a document such as the Bible, it's this group. But I am often astonished at the liberating insights that come from the African American student community and from African American scholars studying the Bible. Pam quoted Itumeleng Mosala, whose life has been involved in the struggle in South Africa. She argues that if you're involved in struggle, you hear struggle in the text. And so those kinds of readings from those kinds of communities are very interesting to me.

SHANKS: I'd like to ask Tikva a question following up on her exposé of allegedly orgiastic Canaanite religion. How would you fit into this picture the enormous number of figurines archaeologists have dug up. They tend to be of two types—one, the rather heavy, large-bellied, big-breasted woman we tend to interpret as a fertility figure, and the other, the slender, curvaceous, often gold figurines from Canaan that emphasize the genitals, not the big breasts of a suckling mother but...

SCHABERG: Two little apples is what you're looking for. (Laughter.)

SHANKS: Right, thank you. How would you fit that into your picture of Canaanite religion?

FRYMER-KENSKY: The large-breasted lady the mother tends to be is, we think, a fertility symbol, in the sense, perhaps, of facilitating childbirth and suckling, nurturing and guarding the child. The erotic figure is no less a fertility figure because she is very much the personification of sexual power in the universe. The sexual act leads, as far as we can tell from Sumerian texts, to agricultural fertility.

Why one was more prominent than the other is a question that, in the absence of texts, is hard to answer. We do know that one of the great preoccupations of Canaanite mythology, as we have it in Ugarit, Syria, in about 1400 B.C.E., is the passing of power from fathers to sons. The rise of the next generation is one of the central dilemmas of patriarchy, how young gods take over from El and El's wife, Asherah, the mother of the gods.

But along with the coming of the new generation into positions of prominence, younger females, perhaps, come into greater cultic use, as witnessed in the figurines, of which we have a few gold ones and some molds, from which thousands of cheap clay ones could be made.

In Israel we don't have these younger female figurines in the biblical period. But it is worth noting what we do have. We have a rather neutral figurine, a figure in the round, with a tree trunk for a bottom and breasts on the torso and a nondescript head, sometimes just a pinch of clay. The essential aspects are the breasts, which has long been noted, and the tree trunk, which has sometimes been mis-seen as a pillar but which definitely flares on the bottom like a tree trunk. This is the lactating, nourishing, nurturing aspect of the universe and may represent what had been meant earlier by Asherah in Israel.

It may also represent God, because what we can see from biblical word-pictures of God is that God is a nongenital, divine being with a beard and breasts. I'm not saying the text actually describes either the beard or the breasts (unless you want to say *Shaddai* has to do with breasts), but God has both the executive powers of the young male and the nurturing and procreative powers of the breasted figure. If we imagine God as a talking torso with beard and breasts or as a great tree connected to the earth, then we wind up with a figure that can go in any direction in terms of gender and sexuality—an infinite possibility of unity. What Western tradition has done with that we all know.

S H A N K S :   Are you saying the Israelite God is depicted in the Bible as genderless?

F R Y M E R - K E N S K Y :   No, sexless.

S H A N K S :   What is its gender?

F R Y M E R - K E N S K Y :   Male. He represents authority. The verbs are always male, and the adjectives are always male, and most of the metaphors, not all, are male. But God is sexless in the sense that the sexuality we find in pagan religions is missing. Absent from the Bible are images of a male God whose potency is located in his upright genitals. There are no hymns to the phallus as a source of fertility, as a source of power. Think, for example, of representations in Greece of the phallus as the great weapon.

So we have a far less sexed figure in the Bible. It's a masculine figure in terms of social order because it reflects the society that conceived of it. When society no longer associates authority with maleness, there is the possibility of understanding God as also gender free.

SHANKS: Does God have feminine characteristics?

FRYMER-KENSKY: That depends on what you mean by feminine characteristics. When God is nurturing and loving and compassionate, is that God the Father or God the Mother? If we say that's God the Mother, then we give men permission not to be compassionate and not to be tender and not to be nurturing. When God is strong and a warrior, is this God as male, or is this the force of disorder that is sometimes associated with a female? Our social structures have decided which characteristics are male and which are female, and we read them into our picture of God.

Certainly the God of the Bible stresses both—God's role in fertility and God's role as tender, compassionate and nurturing, alongside the more classical attribute of forcefulness. We need to remind ourselves that our gendered metaphors are not the only ways of conceiving God. Even in the text, which some of us have been taught is authoritative, we find God the rock, God the tree, God the lion. Hosea is full of metaphors for God that are not just God the husband or God the father, other images of the deity besides biological metaphors.

SHANKS: Hebrew linguistics is full of gender. What about feminine names for God, like Shekhinah?

FRYMER-KENSKY: Yes, in the Bible we get "the one who writhed in labor for you," that is, God writhed in labor for Israel or for humanity. Is that a female image? Is that a male image? Normally we'd say that's a female image. Or the God whose "wombs resonate with tenderness." Male gods in Sumer were called "big of womb," too. Is this a feminine aspect of their being? Or have males co-opted the characteristics of the female and left them with nothing of their own? That's a value judgment.

God is also said to be, in a very ancient poem, the one who bestows the blessings of breasts and wombs. Some male scholars have looked at that and said that must not be God; that must be a vestige of the goddess Asherah who has disappeared from the text. But who says that? The text doesn't say that. It says God gives us the blessings of breasts and wombs.

TRIBLE: The passage you mentioned in Deuteronomy 32:18 —writhing and labor pains giving Israel birth—has traditionally been translated (check the Jerusalem Bible if you want the text) "You forgot the God who *fathered* you." (Chuckles.)

FRYMER-KENSKY: One of the purposes of vernacular translations, as you all know, was to render the Bible accessible. The translators realized that this is a complex text. The preface to the earliest English translation of the Bible, the Tyndale Bible, says specifically that one of the aims is to cast light upon the dark places and simplify what is confusing. You can look at these texts and see where choices have been made to get rid of things that might be troublesome to the patriarchal image, to simplify ambiguities and make women pasteboard figures.

TRIBLE: Yes, the Bible is clearly patriarchal. On that everybody on this panel agrees. But translations have made it worse.

Dr. Schaberg, because of the Beloved Disciple's proximity to Mary Magdalene in John, and because Mary Magdalene is described in Gnostic texts as the one Jesus loved most, and also because the Beloved Disciple threatens Peter and John and Mary does not protest, can Mary Magdalene and the Beloved Disciple be considered one and the same? Have you ever looked at this possibility?

S C H A B E R G :   In an old article, the author—I can't think of the name—proposed something along those lines. If there was some connection in the past, by the time you get to the Fourth Gospel, in the text itself, the Beloved Disciple is male. Male pronouns are used. And he also appears at the crucifixion as a character separate from Mary Magdalene. So there can be no identification there.

I want to ask the panelists about the issue of language, about the fact that the language of religion, both in the Bible and in the Judeo-Christian tradition, is so sexed. The whole concept of a deity is sexed.

F R Y M E R - K E N S K Y :   We need to remind ourselves constantly of this. One way, of course, is to substitute inclusive language. Another way is to substitute, occasionally and randomly, blatantly female language. Still another way is just to keep talking about it.

There is no doubt that the received tradition challenges us. We are supposed to repair the world. We have a broken world, and we have a deeply flawed religious tradition. The job of our generation is to improve it. This has been the job of every generation, but some have ignored it.

But we can no longer ignore the feminist and racist and Eurocentric aspects of our religious tradition. We have read the Bible in a way that has invalidated Asian cultures, for example, but Asian Christians won't accept that any more. They're trying to come up with new ways of synthesizing the Bible and their culture. African American churches are trying to improve the tradition, to nourish groups in struggle, as are oppressed people all over the world. Women and men with an inclusive vision of humanity have to wrestle with God and become heretics in the service of heaven.

Professor Milne, you mentioned Matilda Gage. I read something about her a while ago, just a thumbnail sketch. Am I correct in assuming that she was a leading suffragette in the early days but that she rejected the Bible completely and all organized religion as the single worst enemy of women in the history of the world? Or is that an overstatement?

MILNE: You're asking whether Matilda Gage rejected the Bible and religion as basically the enemy of women and women's rights. Yes, I think that's what set her work apart from the work of the vast majority of 19th-century feminists. She really did see organized religion as a fundamental obstacle that women came up against again and again.

I see the 19th century as much the same as the 20th century, that is, the majority of feminists who look at the Bible—I think that's fairly clear from this panel—still have a positive relationship to it and to organized religion. Most 19th-century feminists stood inside an organized religion. Only a few, like Gage and, I think probably Cady Stanton (by the time she wrote *The Woman's Bible*), rejected the authority of organized religion and the authority of the Bible. Having said that, I don't think you should conclude that they were irreligious.

Wasn't her (Gage's) father a free thinker when she was growing up?

MILNE: You are probably correct, but I have not looked at that part of her life. Let me make a few comments on the previous question, though. You have to distinguish between individual spirituality and organized religion. What early feminists rejected was organized religion and the Bible as the text of organized religion. But they were profoundly religious women in some ways. There weren't a lot of alternatives in those days; there aren't many even today. There aren't many religious/spiritual alternatives for women.

That's what Tikva was talking about earlier. Women are casting about for something to replace this tradition, which has been pervasive in our society. Some women have tried to go back to the ancient goddess traditions and resurrect them, to reclaim them as a basis for women's spirituality. I don't think that can be done. Nor do I think it is the best use of women's energies. We would face all of the problems we face in reclaiming the Bible in a positive way for women, and more. We would have to teach women the basic mythology, to begin with. Then we would have to teach them how to alter it and suppress all the patriarchal stuff in it. It just doesn't seem like a good use of our energy or time to me.

But in the 19th century, it would have been more difficult to have a completely secular point of view. I think Gage and Cady Stanton had a deep sense that organized religion was putting up very serious barriers to women's equality, and they didn't think organized religion was going to change.

I have a question for Miss Trible. What do you make of the claim that the Epistle to the Hebrews may have been written by a woman, possibly a lady called Aquila?

T R I B L E : Although the question is addressed to me, the Second Testament expert is at the other end of the table. So I'll let her respond.

S C H A B E R G : Of all the documents in the Second Testament that have a likely claim, the Epistle to the Hebrews is worth looking at from that angle. Some have suggested that if Prisca (Priscilla) wrote anything, that would be it. She's certainly one of the names that was remembered. I think she is listed three times—twice named before her husband Aquila. And she was known as a teacher. The Epistle to the Hebrews is interesting because it does not favor the creation of a Christian priesthood.

But whether or not we have writing by women in antiquity is difficult, maybe impossible, to judge. A few years ago, some people said they could tell if a woman or a man was playing the piano. (Chuckles.) Virginia Woolf said there was such a thing as a woman's sentence, but we don't really know what that might be. But if any Second Testament document merits being looked at along those lines, the Epistle to the Hebrews would be it.

Bibliography

Albrecht, Gloria. *The Character of Our Communities: Toward an Ethic of Liberation* (Nashville: Abingdon Press, forthcoming).

Atwood, Margaret. *Surfacing* (New York: Simon & Schuster, 1972).

Bach, Alice, ed. *The Pleasure of Her Text: Feminist Readings of Biblical and Historical Texts* (Philadelphia: Trinity Press International, 1990).

Bacon, Margaret Hope. *Mothers of Feminism: The Story of Quaker Women in America* (San Francisco: Harper & Row, 1986).

Bal, Mieke, ed. *Anti-Covenant: Counter-Reading Women's Lives in the Hebrew Bible*, Journal for the Study of the Old Testament Supplement Series 81 (Sheffield, UK: Almond Press, 1989).

———. *Lethal Love: Feminist Literary Readings of Biblical Love Stories* (Bloomington, IN: Indiana University Press, 1987).

Bos, Johanna W.H. and J. Cheryl Exum eds. *Reasoning with the Foxes: Female Wit in a World of Male Power, Semeia* 42 (1988).

Brenner, Athalya, ed. *A Feminist Companion to the Song of Songs* (Sheffield, UK: Sheffield Academic Press, 1993).

Burns, Rita. *Has the Lord Indeed Spoken Only through Moses? A Study of the Biblical Portrait of Miriam*, Society for Biblical Literature Dissertation Series 84 (Atlanta: Scholars Press, 1987).

Camp, Claudia V. *Wisdom and the Feminine in the Book of Proverbs*, Bible and Literature Series 11 (Decatur, GA: Almond Press, 1985).

———. "Woman Wisdom as Root Metaphor: A Theological Consideration" in *The Listening Heart: Essays on Wisdom and Psalms in Honor of Roland E. Murphy*, Kenneth G. Hoglund, Elizabeth F. Huwiler, J. Glass and Robert Lee, eds., JSOTSup 58 (Sheffield, UK: Sheffield Academic Press, 1987).

Christ, Carol. *Diving Deep and Surfacing* (Boston: Beacon Press, 1980)

Christ, Carol, and Judith Plaskow, eds. *Womanspirit Rising: A Feminist Reader in Religion*, (New York: Harper & Row, 1979).

Clark, Elizabeth A., and Herbert W. Richardson, eds. *Women and Religion: A Feminist Sourcebook of Christian Thought* (New York: Harper & Row, 1977).

Clines, David J.A. *What Does Eve Do to Help? And Other Readerly Questions to the Old Testament*, JSOTSup 94 (Sheffield, UK: JSOT Press, 1990).

———. "Why Is There a Song of Songs? And What Does It Do to You If You Read It?" *Jian Dao* 1 (1994).

Collins, Adela Yarbro, ed. *Feminist Perspectives on Biblical Scholarship* (Chico, CA: Scholars Press, 1985).

Craghan, John. "Esther, Judith and Ruth: Paradigms for Human Liberation," *Biblical Theology Bulletin* 12 (1982).

———. "Judith Revisited," *Biblical Theology Bulletin* 12 (1982).

Cross, Frank Moore, Jr., and David Noel Freedman. "The Song of Miriam," *Journal of Near Eastern Studies* 14 (1955).

Curzon, David. "A Hidden Genre: Twentieth-Century Midrashic Poetry," *Tikkun* 9 (1994).

Daly, Mary. *The Church and the Second Sex* (New York: Harper & Row, 1968; with a feminist, post-Christian introduction, 1975).

Davidman, Lynn and Shelly Tenenbaum. *Feminist Perspectives on Jewish Studies* (New Haven: Yale University Press, 1994).

Day, Peggy, ed. *Gender and Difference in Ancient Israel* (Minneapolis: Fortress Press, 1989).

Donaldson, James, and Alexander Roberts, eds. *The Ante-Nicene Fathers: Translations of the Writings of the Fathers Down to A.D. 325* (Grand Rapids, MI: Eerdmans, 1956).

Exum, J. Cheryl. *Fragmented Women: Feminist (Sub)Versions of Biblical Narratives* (Philadelphia: Trinity Press International, 1993).

Exum, J. Cheryl and Johanna W.H. Bos eds. *Reasoning with the Foxes: Female Wit in a World of Male Power. Semeia* 42 (1988).

Fewell, Danna Nolan and David N. Gunn. *Gender, Power, and Promise* (Nashville: Abingdon, 1993).

Flexner, Eleanor. *Century of Struggle: The Women's Rights Movement in the United States*, rev. ed. (Cambridge, MA/London: Harvard University Press, Belknap Press, 1975).

Freedman, David Noel, and Frank Moore Cross, Jr. "The Song of Miriam," *Journal of Near Eastern Studies* 14 (1955).

Friedan, Betty. *The Feminine Mystique* (New York: W.W. Norton, 1963).

Frymer-Kensky, Tikva. *In the Wake of the Goddesses: Women, Culture, and the Biblical Transformation of Pagan Myths* (New York: Macmillan, Free Press, 1992).

———. *The Judicial Ordeal in the Ancient Near East (Styx, October 1995).*

———. *Mother Prayer: A Spiritual Guide to Pregnancy and Childbirth* (New York: Putnam, October 1995).

Fuchs, Esther. " 'For I Have the Way of Women': Deception, Gender and Ideology in the Hebrew Bible," *Semeia* 42 (1988).

———. "Who is Hiding the Truth? Deceptive Women and Biblical Androcentrism" in *Feminist Perspectives on Biblical Scholarship*, ed. Adela Yarbro Collins (Chico, CA: Scholars Press, 1985).

Fulkerson, Mary McClintock. "Contesting Feminist Canons: Discourse and the Problem of Sexist Texts," *Journal of Feminist Studies in Religion 7:2* (1991).

Gage, Matilda Joslyn. *Woman, Church and State: The Original Exposé of Male Collaboration Against the Female Sex* (1893; reprint, Watertown, MA: Persephone Press, 1980).

Gifford, Carolyn De Swarte. "American Women and the Bible: The Nature of Woman as a Hermeneutical Issue" in *Feminist Perspectives on Biblical Scholarship*, ed. Adela Yarbro Collins (Chico, CA: Scholars Press, 1985)

Glass, J., Elizabeth F. Huwiler, Kenneth G. Hoglund and Robert Lee, eds., *The Listening Heart: Essays on Wisdom and Psalms in Honor of Roland E. Murphy* JSOTSup 58 (Sheffield, UK: Sheffield Academic Press, 1987).

Grimké, Sarah. "Letters on the Equality of the Sexes and the Condition of Women," in *The Feminist Papers: From Adams to de Beauvoir*, ed. Alice S. Rossi, (New York/London: Columbia University Press, 1973).

Gunn, David M. and Danna Nolan Fewell. *Gender, Power, and Promise* (Nashville: Abingdon, 1993).

Gurko, Miriam. *The Ladies of Seneca Falls: The Birth of the Women's Rights Movement* (New York: Schocken Books, 1974).

Haskins, Susan. *Mary Magdalene: Myth and Metaphor* (London: HarperCollins, 1993).

Heschel, Susannah. "Anti-Judaism in Christian Feminist Theology," *Tikkun* (May/June 1990).

Hoglund, Kenneth G., Elizabeth F. Huwiler, J. Glass and Robert Lee, eds., *The Listening Heart: Essays on Wisdom and Psalms in Honor of Roland E. Murphy* JSOTSup 58 (Sheffield, UK: Sheffield Academic Press, 1987).

Huwiler, Elizabeth F., Kenneth G. Hoglund, J. Glass and Robert Lee, eds., *The Listening Heart: Essays on Wisdom and Psalms in Honor of Roland E. Murphy* JSOTSup 58 (Sheffield, UK: Sheffield Academic Press, 1987).

James, P.D. *The Children of Men* (New York: Knopf, 1993).

Jay, Nancy. *Throughout Your Generations Forever: Sacrifice, Religion, and Paternity* (Chicago: University of Chicago Press, 1992).

Jobling, David. *The Sense of Biblical Narrative*, Structural Analyses in the Hebrew Bible 2/Journal for the Study of Old Testament Supplement Series 7 (Sheffield, UK: JSOT Press, 1986).

Kinakawa, Hisako. *Women and Jesus in Mark* (Maryknoll, NY: Orbis Books, 1994).

King, Karen L. "The Gospel of Mary" in *The Complete Gospels*, ed. Robert J. Miller (Sonoma CA: Polebridge Press, 1992).

——— . "The Gospel of Mary [Magdalene]" in *Searching The Scriptures: A Feminist Introduction*, vol. 2, (New York: Crossroad, 1994), pp. 601-634.

Kraemer, Ross Shepard. *Her Share of the Blessings: Women's Religions among Pagans, Jews, and Christians in the Greco-Roman World* (New York: Oxford University Press, 1992).

Kramarae, Chris, and Paula Treichler. *A Feminist Dictionary* (Boston: Pandora Press, 1985).

Kramer, H., and J. Sprenger, *Malleus Maleficarum,* tr. Montague Summers (original publication 1486; London, Pushkin Press, 1951),

Lanser, Susan. "(Feminist) Criticism in the Garden: Inferring Genesis 2–3," *Semeia* 41 (1988).

Lee, Robert, J. Glass, Eliazbeth F. Huwiler and Kenneth G. Hoglund, eds., *The Listening Heart: Essays on Wisdom and Psalms in Honor of Roland E. Murphy* JSOTSup 58 (Sheffield, UK: Sheffield Academic Press, 1987).

Lerner, Gerda. *The Creation of Feminist Consciousness* (New York: Oxford University Press, 1993).

———. *The Creation of Patriarchy* (Oxford: Oxford University Press, 1986).

Mack, Burton L. *A Myth of Innocence: Mark and Christian Origins* (Philadelphia: Scholars Press, 1991).

Malvern, Marjorie M. *Venus in Sackcloth* (Carbondale, IL: Southern Illinois University Press, 1975).

Miller, Robert J., ed. *The Complete Gospels* (Sonoma CA: Polebridge Press, 1992).

Milne, Pamela J. "The Patriarchal Stamp of Scripture: The Implications of Structuralist Analysis for Feminist Hermeneutics," *Journal of Feminist Studies in Religion* 5 (1989).

———. "The Patriarchal Stamp of Scripture" in *The Women's Bible Commentary,* Carol Newsom and Sharon Ringe eds. (Philadelphia: Westminster/John Knox, 1992).

———. "What Shall We Do With Judith? A Feminist Reassessment of a Biblical 'Heroine' " *Semeia* 62 (1993).

Mosala, Itumeleng J. "The Implications of the Text of Esther for African Women's Struggle for Liberation in South Africa," *Semeia* 59 (1992).

Murray, Judith Sargent. "On the Equality of the Sexes," (1790), reprinted in Rossi, *The Feminist Papers: From Adams to de Beauvoir* (New York/London: Columbia University Press, 1973).

Newsom, Carol, and Sharon Ringe, *The Women's Bible Commentary.* (Philadelphia: Westminster/John Knox Press, 1992).

Oden, Robert A., Jr., *The Bible Without Theology* (San Francisco: Harper & Row, 1987).

Ostriker, Alicia Suskin. *Feminist Revision and the Bible* (Oxford, UK: Blackwell, 1993).

————. *The Nakedness of the Fathers: Biblical Visions and Revisions* (New Brunswick, NJ: Rutgers University Press, 1994).

Pagels, Elaine. *Adam, Eve and the Serpent* (New York: Random House, 1988).

Phillips, John A. *Eve: The History of an Idea* (San Francisco: Harper & Row, 1984).

Plaskow, Judith. "Anti-Judaism in Feminist Christian Interpretation" in *Searching the Scriptures: A Feminist Introduction*, vol. 1, Elisabeth Schüssler Fiorenza, ed. (New York: Crossroad, 1993).

Plaskow, Judith, and Carol Christ, eds. *Womanspirit Rising: A Feminist Reader in Religion* (New York: Harper & Row, 1979).

Prusak, Bernard P. "Woman: Seductive Siren and Source of Sin" in *Religion and Sexism: Images of Women in Jewish and Christian Traditions*, ed. Rosemary P. Reuther (New York: Simon & Schuster, 1974).

Rabinow, Paul, ed. *The Foucault Reader* (New York: Pantheon Books, 1984).

Reuther, Rosemary P., ed. *Religion and Sexism: Images of Women in Jewish and Christian Traditions* (New York: Simon & Schuster, 1974).

Richardson, Herbert W., and Elizabeth A. Clark, eds. *Women and Religion: A Feminist Sourcebook of Christian Thought* (New York: Harper & Row, 1977).

Ringe, Sharon, and Carol Newsom. *The Women's Bible Commentary* (Philadelphia: Westminster/John Knox Press, 1992).

Roberts, Alexander, and James Donaldson, eds. *The Ante-Nicene Fathers: Translations of the Writings of the Fathers Down to A.D. 325* (Grand Rapids, MI: Eerdmans, 1956).

Rossi, Alice S., ed. *The Feminist Papers: From Adams to de Beauvoir* (New York/London: Columbia University Press, 1973).

Russell, Letty M., ed. *Feminist Interpretations of the Bible* (Philadelphia: Westminster Press, 1985).

Schaberg, Jane. "How Mary Magdalene Became a Whore," *Bible Review*, 8:5 (October 1992).

————. *The Illegitimacy of Jesus: A Feminist Theological Interpretation of the New Testament Infancy Narratives* (San Francisco: Harper San Francisco, 1985).

————. "Thinking Back Through the Magdalene," *Continuum* 1 (1991).

Shanks, Hershel. *Jerusalem: An Archaeological Biography* (New York: Random House, 1995).

————, ed. *The Search for Jesus: Modern Scholarship Looks at the Gospels* (Washington, DC: Biblical Archaeology Society, 1994).

————, ed. *Understanding the Dead Sea Scrolls: A Reader from the Biblical Archaeology Review* (New York: Random House, 1992).

Schüssler Fiorenza, Elisabeth. "Mary Magdalene: Apostle to the Apostles," *Union Theological Seminary Journal* (April 1975).

———. *Searching the Scriptures: A Feminist Introduction*, vol. 1 (New York: Crossroad, 1993).

———. *Searching the Scriptures: A Feminist Introduction*, vol. 2 (New York: Crossroad, 1994).

Sprenger, J., and H. Kramer. *Malleus Maleficarum*, tr. Montague Summers (original publication 1486; London, Pushkin Press, 1951).

Stanton, Elizabeth Cady. *The Woman's Bible* (New York: European Publishing Company, 1895-1898; reprint, Seattle: Coalition Task Force on Women and Religion, 1974).

Tenenbaum, Shelly and Lynn Davidman. *Feminist Perspectives on Jewish Studies* (New Haven: Yale University Press, 1994).

Tolbert, Mary Ann. "Protestant Feminists and the Bible: On the Horns of a Dilemma" in *The Pleasure of Her Text: Feminist Readings of Biblical and Historical Texts*, ed. Alice Bach (Philadelphia: Trinity Press International, 1990).

Treichler, Paula, and Chris Kramarae. *A Feminist Dictionary* (Boston: Pandora Press, 1985).

Trible, Phyllis. "Eve and Adam: Genesis 2-3 Reread" in *Womanspirit Rising: A Feminist Reader in Religion*, ed. Carol Christ and Judith Plaskow (New York: Harper & Row, 1979).

———. *God and the Rhetoric of Sexuality* (Philadelphia: Fortress Press, 1978).

———. "If the Bible's So Patriarchal, How Come I Love It?" *Bible Review* 8:5 (1992).

———. "Postscript: Jottings on the Journey" in *Feminist Interpretations of the Bible*, ed. Letty M. Russell (Philadelphia: Westminster Press, 1985).

———. *Texts of Terror: Literary Feminist Readings of Biblical Narratives* (Philadelphia: Fortress Press, 1984).

Walker, Alice. *In Search of Our Mothers' Gardens: Womanist Prose* (San Diego: Harcourt Brace Jovanovich, 1983).

Williams, Delores S. *Sisters in the Wilderness: The Challenge of Womanist God-Talk* (Maryknoll, NY: Orbis Books, 1993).

Wire, Antoinette Clark. *The Corinthian Women Prophets: A Reconstruction Through Paul's Rhetoric* (Minneapolis: Fortress Press, 1990).

Woolf, Virginia. *Three Guineas* (London: Harcourt Brace Jovanovich, 1938).

Yee, Gale. " 'I Have Perfumed My Bed With Myrrh' ": The Foreign Woman (*'iššâ zārâ*) in Proverbs 1-9, *JSOT* 43 (1989).

Acknowledgments

The Biblical Archaeology Society is grateful to Carol Arenberg, for editing, Laurie Andrews, for copy editing, Judy Wohlberg for production management, and Carla Murphy for transcriptions. Their dedication and expertise were invaluable in preparing this book for publication.